Neanderthal Man

KENNETH A. R. KENNEDY
Cornell University
Ithaca, New York

Discarded
SSCC

Burgess Publishing Company ● Minnea

Copyright © 1975 by Burgess Publishing Company
Printed in the United States of America
Library of Congress Card Number 75-12186
ISBN 0-8087-1116-4

10   9   8   7   6   5   4   3   2   1

A SERIES ON
BASIC CONCEPTS IN ANTHROPOLOGY
Under the Editorship of
A. J. Kelso, University of Colorado
Aram Yengoyan, University of Michigan

For Margaret Miriam Madge Kennedy

Contents

An older conception of Neanderthal man as the typical "cave man" which is no longer accepted by contemporary scientists. Drawing by Charles R. Knight under the direction of Henry Fairfield Osborn (1915). Represented here is Neanderthal man of Le Moustier overlooking the valley of the Vézère, Dordogne, France. (Reprinted from Osborn, 1915)

Discovery of the Neander Valley Fossil

Hairy or grisly, with a big face like a mask, great brow ridges and no forehead, clutching an enormous flint and running like a baboon, with his head forward and not like a man with his head up, he must have been a fearsome creature for our forefathers to come upon.

H. G. Wells 1921

If he could be reincarnated and placed in a New York subway—provided that he were bathed, shaved and dressed in modern clothing—it is doubtful whether he would attract any more attention than some of its other denizens.

W. L. Straus and A.J.E. Cave 1957

These descriptions of Neanderthal man illustrate the conflicting points of view held by popular writers and by scientists, respectively, since the time when a fossilized human skeleton was recovered from a quarry in the Neander Valley of western Germany (Figure 1). The Feldhofer cave exists no more, but before its destruction from mining operations, it was one of several limestone grottos in this vale named in honor of the seventeenth-century composer-poet Joachim Neumann, who wrote under the name "Neander." On a fateful day in August 1856 two workmen encountered some bones which they promptly tossed out of the cave where they had been digging. The foreman gathered up a skullcap and a few of the larger postcranial bones and took them to a high school teacher at nearby Elberfeld. As an instructor of natural science courses and a person familiar with comparative anatomy,

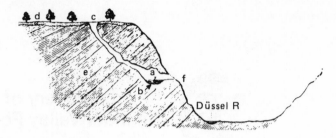

Figure 1. Section of the Neander Valley cave. (a) Cavern 60 feet above the Düssel River, and 100 feet below the surface of the country at c; (b) loam covering the floor of the cave near the bottom of which the human skeleton was found; (b,c) rent connecting the cave with the upper surface of the country; (d) superficial sandy loam; (e) Devonian limestone; (f) terrace, or ledge of rock. (Reprinted from Lyell, 1863)

Johann Karl Fuhlrott recognized that some peculiar features of these bones distinguished them from any human skeletons he had ever before seen. Here was a skull marked with very prominent ridges over the orbits, the forehead was low and narrow, robust bony attachments along the back of the skull testified to its owner's powerful musculature, and the accompanying leg bones were of considerable thickness and degree of curvature. What kind of a creature was this who once inhabited the caves of the Neanderthal (Figure 2)?

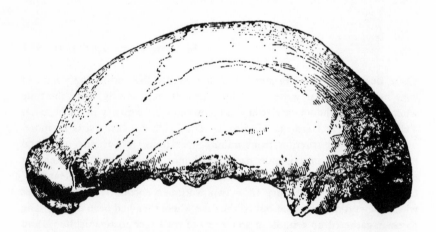

Figure 2. Fossil human skull-cap found at the Neander Valley cave in 1856; 1/2 natural size. (Reprinted from Huxley, 1863)

Overcoming any temptation to retain the bones as an addition to his collection of natural history specimens, Fuhlrott decided to seek the opinion of the eminent anatomist Hermann Schaaffhausen, Professor at the University of Bonn. This authority was impressed indeed by what he was shown, but it was only after several weeks had passed that Schaaffhausen came to realize that the bones were those of a human being. The two men decided to bring this remarkable discovery to the attention of other scientists, an opportunity provided by the meeting of the Lower Rhine Medical and Natural History Society held in Bonn in February of the following year. Meanwhile, Fuhlrott and Schaaffhausen prepared for publication their description and interpretation of the specimen, for they were prepared to argue that the human remains

Belonged to a period antecedent to the time of the Celts and the Germans, and were in all probability derived from one of the wild races of Northwestern Europe, spoken of by the Latin writers.

They asserted that their specimen was that of a normal kind of primitive man, neither a pathologically deformed individual nor an idiot. The massive brow ridges and thick postcranial bones were described as racial characters which were typical of that population which had lived long ago in Germany (Fuhlrott 1859, 1865; Schaaffhausen 1858, 1861.)

Neanderthal man's debut into the scientific world was greeted with rejection, ridicule, and at best, profound misunderstanding of his legitimacy as an earlier kind of man. At the convention at Bonn and later in writings of scientific reports it became apparent that the supporters of the interpretations set forward by Fuhlrott and Schaaffhausen were a small minority. A professor of anatomy at the University of Göttingen attributed the fossils to some "old Dutchman," while a famous French antiquarian was of the opinion that they resembled a robust Celt such as "a modern Irishman with low mental organization." A colleague of Schaaffhausen's argued that those who would have us believe that the protruding brow ridges of the skull were indicative of a primitive and ancient man were deceived, for such are not uncommon features in man today. In fact this professor "had a classmate, who had a brilliant talent for theosophic studies, in whom the eyebrows sprang out far over the pious face." He went on to write that the bones in question must have belonged to an unfortunate sufferer of rickets and arthritis, as demonstrated by an inspection of the pathological abnormalities of the left arm bone, for whom the pain had been so intense and persistent since childhood that the forehead had come to assume a perpetual frown which was eventually imprinted on the bony torus of the skull! This explanation might seem quite sufficient, but this authority added that this whole problem would be cleared up immediately if men of good sense would only recognize that the curved form of the leg bones was indicative of a horseman's lower parts, while the shape of the skull reminded one of a Mongol's head. In short, we have here a rickety Mongolian Cossack soldier who had deserted the army of the Czar when it was driving Napoleon back across the Rhine from Russia in 1814. Overcome with wounds and other miseries, the poor chap sought the refuge of Neander's peaceful valley where he ended his days, a flood later washing his bones into the Feldhofer grotto.

This emphasis upon the anatomical abnormalities of the bones was accepted by other interpreters of the find. A British gentleman who served as the Honorary Secretary of the Anthropological Society of London wrote in 1864 that

All these characters (pathology of the left arm, barrel type of rib box, etc.) are compatible with the Neanderthal skeleton having belonged to some poor idiot or hermit, who died in the cave where his remains have been found. They are incompatible with the evidences which might be left in a West-phalian bone-cave of the remains of a normal healthy uninjured being of the Homo sapiens of Linnaeus.

And in 1872 the same argument was made by the Berlin pathologist Rudolf Virchow who attributed all of the anatomical peculiarities of the Neanderthal specimen to the effects of rickets, arthritis, and several bone-altering thumps on the head. In every other respect, Virchow said, the specimen was a modern-type man of no great antiquity. That these were the vestiges of an individual who had lived into his sixth decade indicated to this medical doctor that here was no primitive representative from a remote age when the life span was brief, particularly for the disabled. Rather this was a citizen of a more enlightened and civilized state wherein the sick and elderly were nursed and not ruthlessly dispatched. This pronouncement from so famous an authority on human ailments satisfied many of the critics of Fuhlrott and Schaaffhausen that the final word had been spoken on the collection of bones from the Neander Valley.

Antediluvian Man

Peripheral to modern views of Neanderthals as this historical account may appear, it nevertheless illustrates the fact that this important fossil had its rebirth into a world whose notions about man's antiquity were very different from those which would be scientifically acceptable today. In this chapter we shall look at some of these now defunct views in order to better understand why Fuhlrott's fossil was considered of dubious value by some of this naturalist's colleagues.

The spectacular advance of the physical sciences in the seventeenth century was followed by investigations into the history of the earth and its inhabitants, areas of inquiry which came under the heading of "Natural History" in the eighteenth century. These pursuits were set apart from the subject matter of the longer established and "more exact" disciplines of physics, chemistry, astronomy, and mathematics. Investigators in all of these areas of knowledge were faithful to their charge of describing the "Laws of Nature" set down by the Creator, a pious task in which the goals of science and religion seemed unopposed. Geologists built theories to account for the history of the earth wherein the events recorded in the *Book of Genesis* were accommodated, albeit often in allegorical form. At the time when Fuhlrott and Schaaffhausen were writing about their skeleton, two geological schools of thought were popular—the thesis of "Catastrophism" favored by French paleontologist Georges Cuvier, and the "Uniformitarian" thesis articulated by the Scots James Hutton and Charles Lyell.

Cuvier professed that there had been a succession of geological worlds, each populated by unique kinds of living things, as demonstrated by the different fossils found in stratified deposits. Each world was separated from previous and succeeding ones by periodic cataclysms when fire and flood erased earlier landscapes and established new ones. A few animal and plant species survived each catastrophe to begin the population of the next world. In this nonevolutionary scheme, species were considered to be biologically fixed, i.e., the various biotic kinds were immutable from the moment of their special creation. The biblical Deluge was man's account of the last destructive episode. Cuvier rejected any suggestion that mankind had lived through prior catastrophes, save perhaps in Asia, the reputed cradle of the human race. While accepting the fossil evidence for ancient kinds of life of which some species had become extinct, Cuvier was adamant in rejecting claims for fossil man. Not surprisingly, this account of geological events found favor among those scientists and laymen of the first half of the nineteenth century who adhered to the *Genesis* account of man's origin. While conceding to the probability that some lines of animals and plants had antiquities of many millenia, they could not conceive that man had been on earth for more than six thousand years.

Uniformitarian geologists, whose influence became apparent after 1830, rejected the thesis of catastrophic cycles. Rather, they regarded natural agencies modifying the world of the past to be no different in essence or degree from those operating in the world today. Their enthusiasm in assigning a profound antiquity to the earth and their indifference to the incorporation of biblical chronologies into their writings earned them the charges of atheism and materialism by more orthodox folk who were concerned about the encroachment of science upon the domain of religious interpretations of Creation. When the Swiss geologist Louis Agassiz published in 1840 his arguments for the existence of glacial activity in Europe and North America, geological formations which had been attributed to floods became more readily conceivable as the consequences of periodic action of ice accumulations and glacial movements. The older terms "diluvium," "antediluvium," and "drift" lost their significance in the study of those earth changes taking place during the Ice Age or the Pleistocene, as this geological epoch is called today. Glacial advances were an important feature of the latter half of the Pleistocene, i.e., within the past one million years. But in 1856 the significance of the new geology was only partially perceived, particularly on the European continent where Cuvier's influence persisted for a longer time than it did in England and America.

Because of the assumption that man is a newcomer to earth, a number of discoveries of bones of prehistoric man were rejected in the years preceding the date of the Neander Valley find. As early as 1774 a priest reported that he had come upon some human bones buried in the vicinity of a bear skeleton at Gailenreuth near Bamberg, southern Germany. But he could not decide whether

They belong to a Druid or to an Ante-diluvian or to a Mortal Man of more recent times....I dare not presume without sufficient reason these human members to be of the same age as the other animal petrifactions. They must have got there by chance with them.

The Gailenreuth discovery was rejected by the leading naturalists of that time as either the bungled work of an amateur who had mixed recent human bones with those of more ancient animals, or the result of human remains having fallen into a deeper and earlier deposit which was the proper context of the extinct fauna.

Explanations of this sort were evoked in later situations where human bones were found in association with the remains of extinct species of cave bear, rhinoceros, mammoth, hyena, and reindeer. Assemblages of this nature were found at Köstritz and Bilzingsleven in central Germany between 1820 and 1922, at Lahr in the Rhine Valley near Freiberg a year later, at Engis and Engihoul near Liège on the banks of the Meuse in Belgium, and in France in Aude in 1828, Pondres and Souvignarques in Gard in 1829, and in the Herhault caves in 1838. Sometimes the arguments against man's great antiquity and contemporaneity with extinct animals were ingeniously contrived, as in the case of a Dean of Westminster's fantasy that a human burial encountered in 1823 in a fossiliferous cave at Goat's Hole near Paviland, Wales, was the skeleton of a female practitioner of the oldest profession who serviced the soldiers of a Roman military settlement, the ruins of which could be seen in the immediate vicinity of the cave. Dean Buckland was a chief advocate of Cuverian catastrophic geology in England. Many years later a reexamination of the "Red Lady of Paviland" (so called because the bones were painted with red ochre) showed that the skeleton was a fine specimen of prehistoric times which predated the Roman invasion of England by some 18,000 years!

Only half of these collections of ancient human remains which were encountered before the time of the 1856 discovery of Neanderthal man have survived to the present day for our reevaluation of them as sound evidence that our ancestors were living at the same period of time as did the extinct creatures whose fossils shared their graves. Those specimens not preserved became lost or were in some instances intentionally destroyed, so threatening was their existence to the tenet that fossil man was an impossibility.

In fairness to the doubters, we must recognize that two very important problems inhibited the rapid development of human paleontology as a field of natural science prior to 1856. In the first place, researches into the prehistoric archeological record were not sufficiently advanced to allow scholars to assign the prehistoric stone tools and the faunal and human bones found with them to an absolute time scale measurable in the passing of solar years. Even the working out of a relative sequence of archaeological specimens into an Age of Stone, a Bronze Age, and an Iron Age sequence, as was initiated by Danish prehistorians in the 1830s, did not solve the chronological issue of how old an artifact or a bone might be. This dilemma was expressed by the founder of the prehistoric collections at the Danish National Museum:

Everything which has come down to us from heathendom is wrapped in a thick fog; it belongs to a space of time we cannot measure. We know that it is older than Christendom, but whether by a couple of years or a couple of centuries, or even by more than a millenium, we can do no more than guess.

Until more accurate dating methods of modern geology, chemistry, and physics were applied to this problem, ancient times were divisible only into a recent period of written accounts and an earlier preliterate period. The Deluge of biblical tradition marked a convenient division of antiquity into an antediluvian and a postdiluvian period. But there seemed to be no way to avoid the problem of apparent contemporaneity of most prehistoric remains. The terms "Celtic," "Anglo-Saxon," "Gallic," "Druidical," and the like blanketed everything earlier than Roman times in western Europe.

This brings us to the second problem. Some of the announcements of discoveries of antediluvian man justifiably met derision from scientists for the reason that the bones exhibited as proof of this claim were often not human bones at all. A notable case was the proclamation of the finding of an "old sinner" from the Deluge whose reputed remains turned up in Switzerland. However, subsequent examination of the bones revealed that their true identity was a Mesozoic fossil reptile of the genus *Ichthyosaurus.* The champion of this relic, which was limited to a couple of vertebrae, was a Zurich naturalist, Johann Jacob Scheuchzer. He wrote a thesis entitled *The Grievances and Claims of the Fishes* wherein the antediluvian status of the vertebrae was pressed. In this curious work, scholars who attributed fossils to circumstances other than the Deluge were engaged in debate by irate fishes whose fate was affected by the human folly that brought about their "death by drowning" in that watery holocaust. Not discouraged by his critics, Scheuchzer put forward another group of bones found at Oeningen near Constance in *A Most Rare Memorial of That Accursed Generation of Men of the First World, the Skeleton of a Man Drowned in the Flood,* as the translation of the title of his paper of 1726 has been rendered. In a later treatise he described the skeleton in some detail concluding with the couplet,

Affected skeleton of old, doomed to damnation,
Soften, thou stone, the hearts of this wicked generation.

(Translated by H. Wendt)

Alas, Scheuchzer was mistaken again, for the Oeningen specimen turned out to be a fossil giant salamander dating to a period of some 15 million years ago!

Naive claims of this order did not advance the cause of that small group of naturalists who favored the view that fossils of ancient man might one day be found. Thus it was that the discovery of Neanderthal man did not result immediately in the penetration of this fog which obscured knowledge of the true relationships of early traces of our ancestors and the bones of extinct animals found with him, for neither geological stratigraphy nor artifactual and faunal associations were preserved during the quarrying operations at the Feldhofer cave.

Early Scientific Evidence for Man's Antiquity and Evolution

Events which led to recognition of the fossil evidence of man's antiquity began with archeological discoveries. Stone tools were unearthed beside the bones of extinct mammals. This kind of association, rather than one in which human bones were found with remains of extinct fauna, gradually forced nineteenth-century writers about prehistoric life to admit that man had been the contemporary of some of the extinct beasts, as we shall see in this brief survey of the early days of human paleontology. Here we must ask the question, how was the great antiquity of man first established on the basis of scientific evidence?

By the middle of the eighteenth century most educated people had abandoned the notion that the regularly-shaped stone and metal artifacts found in fields and streambeds were produced by electrical storms and possessed supernatural powers. Instead it seemed obvious that many of these "lightning stones" were similar in form to implements made by American Indians and by other contemporary populations with primitive technologies. But the older interpretations did not disappear overnight. In 1715 a London apothecary and antique dealer by the name of Conyers found a stone axe in a deposit containing mammoth bones which had been dredged from the Thames River. He concluded that the creature had been slain by this very weapon by some ancient Briton, but he was ridiculed so ruthlessly that he conceded to the safer view that the axe was not of great antiquity after all and that the giant animal was in fact one of the elephants brought to England by the Roman army during the reign of Claudius! Similarly, some stone tools found with extinct animals by John Frere in Suffolk in 1797 were rejected when he suggested that

The situation in which these weapons were found may tempt us to refer them to a very remote period indeed; even beyond that of the present world.

John McEnery, a priest, dug at Kent's Cavern, Torquay, in 1825 after the deposit had been disturbed by antiquarians seeking a Mithraic temple. Here he found flint implements associated with fossil rhinoceros bones under an unbroken floor of stalagmite. He continued his investigations for fifteen years despite rejection of his evidence of prehistoric man's contemporancity with extinct fauna by leading naturalists of his day. In deference to Dean Buckland's strong opinions on the subject, McEnery did not publish his researches. They were published posthumously. The Dean of Westminster had again imposed his Cuverian view, as he had earlier with the "Red Lady of Paviland."

A similar story could be told on the Continent where M. Jouannet in 1810 and M. Tournal in the late 1820s and early 1830s were excavating in southern France. At this same time P. C. Schmerling, an anatomist at the University of Liège, conducted explorations of over forty caverns in Belgium. Few educated people were willing to listen to the claims of these men regarding man's intimate association with ancient and extinct animals. Then in 1836 Boucher de Perthes, a customs inspector at the town of Abbeville, France, discovered some flint axes from ancient beds of the Somme River. Although his descriptions of these finds were not taken seriously by his contemporaries, he continued to work alone, and published in 1846 the initial volume of his *Antiquités celtiques et antédiluviennes* wherein he announced that

In spite of their imperfections, these rude stones prove the existence of [antediluvian] man as surely as a whole Louvre would have done.

De Perthes did not find human bones with his assemblages of stone tools and fossil fauna as Tournal and Schmerling had done, but his writings provided the catalyst for a change of opinion among the leading naturalists of England and the Continent regarding man's antiquity.

This important development came about when de Perthes won the support of a distinguished physician and compatriot, a Dr. Rigollot of Amiens, who viewed the disputed evidence himself at first hand and went on to discover a number of ancient tools at St. Acheul, a suburb of Amiens. The work of Rigollot was brief, for in the following year, 1855, he died and de Perthes was alone once again. But more and more French antiquarians were becoming interested in the finds and interpretations of the customs officer, and when the British paleontologist Hugh Falconer passed through Abbeville in 1859 on his way to Sicily, he too was impressed by what he saw and with the meticulous efforts of de Perthes. Falconer arranged for the visits of several eminent British geologists to Abbeville, and later in this same year of 1859 a paper was read by one of these visitors to the assembly of educated elite at the Royal Society, London. Here claims of de Perthes and Rigollot were upheld, and this approval by so august a body swayed scientific opinion in other countries. Meanwhile, McEnery's earlier work at Kent's Cavern was vindicated by excavations carried out in an undisturbed cave deposit at Brixham and also in Devonshire. Here flint tools were uncovered in association with bones of ancient animals from a deposit sealed from above by a layer of solid limestone.

During this period when the question of man's antiquity was being resolved through British acceptance of the French lithic evidence, Neanderthal man had been known for some three years to members of the scientific community. However, as we have noted, claims for the discovery of the bony remains of early man were still being rejected. Without benefit of careful excavation, or even lithic and faunal associations, the Neander Valley skeleton seemed but one more piece of insubstantial evidence of fossil man. It was a very different event in that fateful year of 1859 which forced Neanderthal man to the forefront of everyone's attention—the publication of the volume entitled *On the Origin of Species by Means of Natural Selection, or the Preservation of Favoured Races in the Struggle for Life* by the British naturalist Charles Darwin.

While Darwin did not mention Neanderthal man in this book (indeed he carefully avoided references to the biological history of mankind and only indirectly noted the implications of this theory of organic evolution by natural selection to our species), the point was made that living things must have been on the earth far longer than chronologies based upon the few thousand years of Creationist speculation would allow. Life must be very ancient if the primary mechanism of the evolutionary process, natural selection, could explain the variety of adaptations we see in biotic forms and the modification of anatomical structures of living species by their descent from earlier forms. By rejecting the tenet of species immutability and special Creation, and by offering a plausible theory of how evolution operates as a natural process, Darwin opened the door to other scientists interested in establishing the true scope of man's antiquity and biological affinities between contemporary and ancient forms of life. Forerunners of Darwin, while favoring evolution as a theory, had failed to account for how species could be modified over time, nor was their documentation of evolution through exhaustive research and observation of sufficient weight to carry the force of an argument about evolutionary processes.

The problem of man's origins and duration of time on earth was faced by the Uniformitarian geologist Charles Lyell whose book *The Geological Evidence of the Antiquity of Man* was published in 1863. He reviewed the evidence for the discoveries of human bones, giving particular attention to the Neander Valley skeleton and to an earlier discovery of human remains from the Engis grotto in Belgium. He refuted the notions that these bones were recent and intrusive in earlier deposits or that their association with the faunal remains was real but that the animals were of species which had survived into more recent times.

The matter of man's biological relationships to other animals, especially to the anthropoid apes, was the topic of Thomas Huxley's famous collection of essays also published in 1863, *Evidence as to Man's Place in Nature.* As a comparative anatomist, Huxley stressed the importance of homologous structures in man and ape, but he also required some fossil evidence to document the thesis that mankind had changed over time and that our ancestors had anatomical characters which were more primitive (apelike) than those exhibited by human beings today. Neanderthal man was of crucial importance to this champion of Darwinian evolution, for Huxley was all too aware that his critics would demand proof of a "missing link" in the fossil record if the theory of evolution had any relevance to our species.

A plaster-of-Paris cast of the Neander Valley skull had been turned over to Huxley by Lyell who had brought it from Germany and had for a time exhibited it in London. When we read Huxley's essays today we may be puzzled as to why he shifts from interpreting the Neanderthal specimen as very primitive—"Under whatever aspect we view this cranium... we meet with ape-like characters, stamping it as the most pithecoid of human crania yet discovered"— to a position in which the skull's modern anatomical features are emphasized, as when he indicates its place as "An extreme term in a series leading gradually from it to the highest and best developed of human crania." Huxley was aware of the many anatomical features of the specimen which fall within the normal range of variation for modern man: cranial capacity (about 1230 cc. which is near the mean for Hottentot skulls), cranial robusticity (like a rugged male skull from the Neolithic Borreby site in Denmark and Australian aboriginal crania), limb dimensions and proportions (as in modern Europeans of average stature), and limb bone robusticity (as found in Patagonian natives). Therefore he was unwilling to push too hard a claim that the Neander Valley specimen is the missing link between ape and man. Many years were to pass before more ancient and anatomically different kinds of human ancestors were discovered, so to this extent Neanderthal man was a disappointment to those early evolutionists seeking a particular kind of paleontological evidence to support their thesis that man had ancestral roots in an anthropoid stock. It is not surprising then that Huxley and his immediate successors stressed the pithecoid features of Neanderthals, and in the absence of more ancient human fossils, looked to modern anthropoid ape and human populations for comparative data. Here lies a fundamental reason for Neanderthal man's reputation as a brutish kind of human ancestor, a theme later elaborated by some anthropologists, as we shall see.

In summary, we have seen in the last two chapters how certain developments within the sciences of geology, Darwinian evolutionary biology, and comparative anatomy contributed to the scientific respectability of the idea of fossil man. At the same time, the research of prehistoric archeologists was establishing procedures for measuring the duration of time man had existed on the earth, and accumulating the artifactual record which would become the basis for interpretation of the lifeways of our ancient ancestors. Only after some progress had been made in these fields of study could the fossil from the Neander Valley be properly evaluated as to its scientific importance.

 **Establishing the Fossil Record**

Among the finds of ancient men which were discovered before 1856 was a skull with face, upper jaw, and dentition from Forbes' Quarry on the island of Gibraltar. It is first mentioned in the minutes of the Gibraltar Scientific Society dated 1848 and seems to have turned up during the repair of fortifications on the North Front of the rock. Some sixteen years later the governor of the military prison on Gibraltar presented the specimen to the anatomist George Busk who had it displayed at the meeting of the British Association for the Advancement of Science at Bath. Thereafter it was stored away in the museum of the Royal College of Surgeons for some fifty years without attracting much attention. This neglect of the Gibraltar skull is curious, for it rather than the Neander Valley specimen is actually the first discovery of a member of that extinct population we now call Neanderthal. Its similarity to Fuhlrott's skeleton was not deemed important until the early part of the present century, although Busk did note some of its resemblances. Falconer observed that

It is a case of a very low type of humanity—very low and savage, and of extreme antiquity—but still man, and not a half-way step between man and monkey.

In short, it is another disqualified candidate for a missing link.

Lower jaws were not preserved with either the Neander Valley or Forbes' Quarry specimens. When a Belgian prehistorian found in 1866 a mandible, canine tooth, and some hand bones in the cavern of Trou de la Naulette in Namur, controversy was stirred over the significance of the find. Although removed from a deep deposit amidst fossils of mammoth, rhinoceros, and reindeer, a situation that would certainly seem to silence scepticism as to the age of the human remains, Virchow's voice was heard once more raised in protest. There were no stone tools found with the collection of bones, he noted. The fact that the mandible was chinless delighted those scientists seeking proof of man's evolution in the fossil record, for such would be a critical hallmark of ape status, but to the great Prussian pathologist this character was not significant. Fourteen years later Virchow contested the authenticity of another fossil mandible, this one from the Šipka cave in what is now Czechoslovakia. This is a very robust jaw with a dental complement indicating it belonged to a ten-year-old child, probably a boy. But to its chief critic it was a pathological specimen of quite recent times. The association of Pleistocene fauna and stone tools did not influence Virchow. However, by the time the Šipka specimen was being discussed by the larger scientific community, Virchow's influence as disclaimer of fossil man was on the decline. Today the La Naulette and Šipka mandibles are regarded as legitimate specimens of Neanderthal man, as was a mandible found in 1859 at Arcy-sur-Cure in France.

It was the discovery in 1886 of two skeletons having cranial features similar to the Neander Valley specimen that finally settled the arguments about Neanderthal man's antiquity and acceptance as a human ancestor. In the Spy caverns of Belgium, not far from the find site of the La Naulette mandible, the human bones were uncovered in direct association with glacial fauna, namely woolly rhinoceros and mammoth. Also found here were stone tools of a type known to be later in time of manufacture than those collected by de Perthes on the Somme. While the Somme gravels yielded handaxes assigned to the Chellean industry, the Spy artifacts are flake tools of a complex which came to be called "Mousterian." These associations, plus the fact that the excavation at Spy was conducted with precision by trained personnel convinced many scientists who had been sceptical of the earlier evidence for fossil man that it was time to change their minds.

Since the time of this remarkable discovery, fossils identified as Neanderthals have been found elsewhere in Belgium and Germany as well as in the other western European countries of France, Spain, and Italy. A second Neanderthal specimen was later found on Gibraltar. While no Neanderthals are known thus far from England, Jersey, in the Channel Islands, has yielded fossil evidence. In addition to the Šipka find, Neanderthal bones have been found elsewhere in Czechoslovakia and in other central European countries of Hungary, Rumania, Yugoslavia and in the U.S.S.R. as far eastward as Crimea and Uzbekistan. Many anthropologists would include as Neanderthals certain fossils from the Near Eastern countries of Turkey, Israel, Lebanon, Syria, Iraq, Iran, and Afghanistan. Neanderthal remains have not been found in Arabia, India, or Pakistan. Sites in Libya and Morocco in North Africa have yielded bones that some scholars would identify as belonging to Neanderthals, but there are grounds for excluding certain fossil hominid finds of eastern and southern Africa and of Southeast Asia from the Neanderthal series, as we shall discuss below.

A census of skeletal specimens which have been labeled Neanderthal by anthropologists was published in 1962 (Coon 1962). Some eighty-two skeletal specimens from forty-two sites of the Würm I glacial period were listed. Specimens from Europe were counted with other so-called Neanderthals from western and central Asia. While we might not agree that all of the entries on this register are appropriate, the count does provide some notion of the size of the skeletal data available for our scrutiny.

Names for Neanderthals

In a letter Falconer wrote to Busk just before the meeting of the British Association in 1864, he proposed that the Gibraltar skull be given the scientific name of *Homo calpicus,* "Calpe" being the ancient name for Gibraltar. Had this letter been written and published a little earlier, it would have been the basis for naming the Neander Valley specimen and all others presumably related to it according to Falconer's title. But it fell to William King, an anatomy professor at Queen's College, Galway, Ireland, to christen the skull with the name that has taxonomic priority—*Homo neanderthalensis.* King made this announcement at the British Association meeting held in Newcastle in 1863, and the following year the report was published. This specimen appeared to King to be too apelike to resemble man today, hence a species taxon seemed appropriate. By the time the Germans got around to naming their national treasure *Homo primigenius* in 1898, it was too late for this title to win recognition from the scientific community because initial taxonomic names have priority by international agreement. The Neander Valley specimen is called the "holotype" of all other discoveries of fossils identified as Neanderthals since this was the single specimen designated by an author as the type of a species or lower taxon at the time of establishing the biotic group.

Other names proposed for Neanderthals, frequently by discoverers and describers of new finds, have suffered a like fate of oblivion. These include *Homo europaeus, Homo antiquus,* and *Homo mousteriensis.* Similarly, colloquial terms have failed to receive universal recognition, as when some French anthropologists of the last century argued that Neanderthals belonged to the "Cannstadt race," a reference to some human remains of uncertain antiquity which had been found in 1700 near Stuttgart, Germany.

Among those contemporary anthropologists who would not assign Neanderthals to a species different from our own, the name *Homo sapiens* seems proper, but with the trinomial tag of *neanderthalensis* to distinguish this ancient group from ourselves and our immediate ancestors, *Homo sapiens sapiens.* Implicit in this is the declaration that the anatomical variables of this extinct population are not markers of great biological distance separating Neanderthals from man today. Rather, anatomical differences are of a relative order of racial differences found in the single species of mankind today. However, the notion that Neanderthals were not sapient hominids persists among some contemporary scholars who adhere to King's original taxon, and imply thereby that Neanderthals were reproductively isolated from prehistoric *sapiens* populations.

Estimation of biological distance is of importance to students of the paleontological record. Unfortunately, the morphology of mineralized bones and of teeth is not a completely trustworthy guide to revealing the existence of reproductive isolation. Only with living things is it possible to carry out the kinds of breeding experiments which will assist the taxonomist in deciding whether two kinds of organisms should be assigned to the same or to different species. Fossils have long since passed their capacity to assist us with procedures of this sort! Therefore paleontologists must base their evaluations of biological distance upon the importance they assign to morphological variations, recognizing that this procedure has its limitations. Taxonomic names reflect these evaluations. In situations where the fossil record of an organism is relatively full, the taxonomist can often form conclusions about a species' variability and affinity to other species with a higher level of confidence than in cases where an ancient population is recognized by only a few specimens, or when the organism in question is of a sort not known from a number of find sites.

Apart from species, which may be defined by the criterion of known or assumed reproduction isolation, none of the higher categories of the taxonomic hierarchy from species to genera, families, orders, classes, phyla, and kingdoms (and all subdivisions of these) can be thought of as natural entities. Man himself imposes a classification upon nature: living things do not evolve with intrinsic taxonomic labels which it is the task of the systematist to reveal! Hence changes in the taxonomic status of an extinct or living group of organisms may occur as more information is gained as to its affinities to related forms. To understand how Neanderthals have been classified is to better appreciate the place anthropologists have given them in the story of man's biological history.

The method of classifying living nature which is in use today by biologists has its historical roots in the eighteenth century when a Swedish naturalist, Carolus Linnaeus, prepared the volumes of his great work, *Systema Naturae.* In its tenth edition in 1758, man is classified as a member of the order Primates along with prosimians, monkeys, apes, and some monsters which were omitted from later editions edited by Linnaeus' students. Linnaeus himself assigned man to a separate genus, *Homo,* and to the species name *sapiens.* He included four subspecific divisions of mankind for the races of Europe, Africa, Asia, and the Americas. A fifth subspecies was *Homo sapiens ferus,* or wild man, an entry dropped from later editions of his work. While Linnaeus was fascinated in his later years with the notion that species might be mutable and have the capacity to undergo changes which we would today call evolutionary, his taxonomic system was itself a static one, the species being essentially primal forms as originally created by God. It was Cuvier who added extinct species to Linnaean taxonomy many years later, and it was Darwin who rendered the scheme dynamic and temporal through his arguments for the origin and evolution of species.

Later we shall encounter some other taxonomic and colloquial names for Neanderthals and their kin, discovering that "Neanderthal" means different things to different scholars looking at the problems of this group's origins, ancestral lines, and affinities to man today. But now a final word on the name itself. By the rules of the International Code of Zoological Nomenclature, the scientific name *neanderthalensis* must retain its letter *h,* even though this has been dropped in the modern German spelling of "Tal" (valley) and in a number of other words spelled earlier with the *h,* proper names for families and towns usually excepted. It has become very much a matter of individual taste among writers of English whether to write "Neanderthal" or "Neandertal", but in any case the sound "th" is dropped from pronounciation in both forms.

Frameworks for Establishing Antiquity

By the early decades of the present century the richness of the Neanderthal fossil record made it apparent to many anthropologists that all discovery sites had these three features in common: (1) faunal and geological associations of an antiquity datable to the period of time just prior to and during the final glacial advance in Europe—the Würm glaciation; (2) cultural associations belonging to the technological industry called Mousterian; (3) anatomical similarities in the human skeletal remains which distinguished these specimens from anatomically modern *Homo sapiens* who make their initial appearance during the latter part of the Würm glaciation in Europe. In this section we shall look more closely at the first two issues, and discuss the third topic in the sections which follow.

Although the Pleistocene was equated with the Ice Age in earlier geological accounts, we know today that the major glacial events took place only within the final phases of the epoch which began some three million years ago. There is some evidence of glacial activity during this earlier part of the Pleistocene, a division of time called the Villafranchian, as well as during some pre-Pleistocene epochs of earth history. It is the more recent accumulation of ice in the northern hemisphere and in high altitude regions to the south which is of interest to us here. Geologists do not agree on the causes of glacial phenomena; arguments rest upon theories that changes in solar radiation affecting our planet were due to perturbation of the earth's axis, precessions of the equinox, or alterations of the orbital pathway of the earth. But the evidence of periods of glacial advances and retreats is well documented from studies of sea cores, river and beach levels, and paleontology.

Four periods of major glacial optima have been established for Europe, Eurasia, and North America when one-third of the earth's surface was covered with ice. At the peak of each glaciation, sea levels lowered thus enlarging continental and island landmasses as well as providing landbridges in regions of shallow seas. Rates of precipitation fluctuated correspondingly in lands peripheral to glaciated regions. In Africa, episodes of intense rainfall, called "pluvials," alternated with dry "interpluvial" periods, but the precise correlation of glacial and pluvial phenomena remains uncertain. Valley glaciers formed in high altitude areas as far away from the places of ice sheet concentration as Peru, Australia, and New Zealand, but once more, exact correspondence of valley glaciers in the southlands with ice sheets in the northern hemisphere has not been possible.

Pleistocene glaciations were described in 1900 by geologists studying the Alps where evidence of river terraces and moraines indicated that ice had accumulated and retreated more than once within the geologically recent history of this mountain region. Four glacial events were identified, each bearing the name of the local Alpine region where investigations had been conducted: Günz, Mindel, Riss, and Würm. In this series the Günz glaciation, while considered more local in effect than subsequent ice advances, was held to be the earliest while the Würm was the latest. Between each of these cold and wet climatic conditions, somewhat warmer periods occurred, marked by the retreat of the ice with consequent elevation of sea levels. These deglaciated and more temperate periods are called "interglacials" of which there are three: Günz-Mindel or Cromerian, Mindel-Riss or Hoxnian, and Riss-Würm or Eemian. These are also known as the first, second, and third interglacials. This Alpine scheme has been extended to parts of Europe, Eurasia, and North America, although the glacial advances are known by different regional names. As more was learned about glacial geology, it came to be recognized that there had been minor climatic fluctuations within each of the major glacial optima, periods of slight deglaciation with some warming of paleotemperatures, to be followed again by the onset of colder conditions. These alterations are called "interstadials" and "stadials" for warmer and colder periods, respectively. For a given glacial advance, these subsidiary events are referred to by Roman numerals—Würm I, Würm II, Würm III. These too are known by regional names (Figure 3).

What is important to understand is that fossil men whom we would recognize as Neanderthals made their first appearance in Europe during the Riss-Würm interglacial, that is from 150,000 to 75,000 years ago. Neanderthals became the dominant population over much of Europe in the period of Würm I, and continued to survive through the Würm I-II interstadial which began some 60,000 years ago. But by the dawn of Würm III times they had disappeared. After 40,000 years ago, modern-type men had come into possession of the areas formerly occupied by Neanderthals and had begun settlement of new areas, such as the Americas and Australia. Passage to these continents was made possible by the lowering of sea levels so that landbridges

Figure 3. Schematic curve representing undulations of the Würm glaciation in Europe, showing the main phases of loess deposition (stippled), the current terminology, and radiocarbon chronology. (Reprinted from Kenneth P. Oakley, *Framework for Dating Fossil Man* [George Weidenfeld & Nicolson Ltd., London, England, 1964]; copyright © 1964 by Kenneth P. Oakley. Reprinted by permission of the author and Aldine Publishing Company)

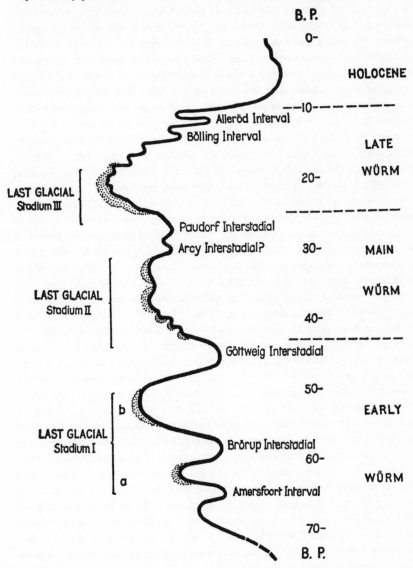

were formed. Although there is a comforting fiction that the Pleistocene is passed and that we have been living for the past ten millenia in a subsequent geological epoch called the "Holocene" or "Recent," many geologists insist that we are presently enjoying an interglacial period which may well come to an end in a few thousand years with the onset of renewed glacial activity. The sword of Damocles may be suspended over us!

Glacial and pluvial periods provide convenient time markers for scientists studying such Pleistocene events as the migrations of animal and plant species, formation and disappearance of landbridges, and the influence of the geoclimatic changes upon the food resource base, ecological adaptations, and habitation areas of prehistoric man. The dating of geological and paleontological events of this time has also provided us with a relative chronology for assessing the antiquity of deposits, as when we can assign some early Neanderthals to the Riss-Würm interglacial by their direct association with remains of *Elephas antiquus,* while later Neanderthals of Würm I times are commonly found with the mammoth species that replaced it, *Elephas primigenius.* Other "index fossils" of the time when Neanderthals lived in Europe are Merck's rhinoceros and hippopotamus living in pine and oak forests along with deer, wolf, and boar at the beginnings of Würm I. These animals were replaced by the woolly rhinoceros, horse, and wild cattle in open lands as the intense cold of this stadial reached its maximum. By Würm II times reindeer had become a predominant occupant of Europe. These environmental changes are also seen from studies of fossil soils and pollens which have important implications for methods of relative dating.

For absolute dating of past geoclimatic deposits where the passing of solar years is counted, laboratory analysis of samples of organic content and rocks has been done in which rates of isotopic alterations are counted. The methods most frequently used today in studies of early man are those of radiocarbon, potassium-argon, uranium-lead, fission-track dating, and a number of others less well known, the choice of method being determined by the presumed degree of antiquity of the specimen under consideration. Other absolute dating methods include counting tree rings, counting soil depositions, and noting shoreline accumulations. One well-supported date expressed in solar years must be established in dating these sequences. Some methods cannot be extended backwards in time to more than a few millenia. Most relative and absolute dating methods used for paleonthological and archeological deposits are established upon one or a variety of procedures which analyze physical-chemical properties, geochronology, or the nature of plant and animal remains. The archeologist may use additional dating techniques based upon stylistic changes of artifacts, calendrical records, rates of accumulation of refuse, and cross-dating of artifacts in separate geographical regions.

The technological tradition dated to the Riss-Würm interglacial and the early and middle divisions of the Würm glaciation is called Mousterian. It was so named in 1867 by the archeologist Gabriel de Mortillet with reference to the Neanderthal cave site of Le Moustier in the Dordogne Valley of France where flake tools of a distinctive pattern were first found in abundance. In time the Mousterian "stage" of technological development was established as one of a series of cultural subdivisions of the "Old Stone Age," or "Paleolithic." More specifically, the Mousterian was held to be the hallmark of the "Middle Paleolithic," earlier subdivisions being the "Chellean" and "Acheulian" periods of the Lower Paleolithic while an Upper Paleolithic was represented by tool technologies called "Aurignacian," "Solutrean," and "Magdalenian." Tools of the early part of this technological evolutionary scheme were of the kind de Perthes had collected, namely handaxes and cleavers made on cores of rocks. Middle Paleolithic (Mousterian) tools were quite different, being chipped from flakes and then retouched along the flake margins to form a cutting plane (Figure 4). The tool kit of the Upper Paleolithic included parallel-sided flakes or blades plus elaborately worked implements of such nonlithic materials as ivory, antler, and bone. It was in the context of this Upper Paleolithic tradition that populations of modern-type *Homo sapiens* produced cave paintings in southwestern Europe and rendered artistic carvings in ivory and bone here and in eastern Europe.

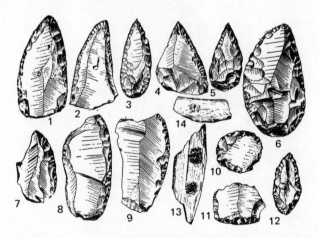

Figure 4. Mousterian implements of flint and bone from La Ferrassie. Nos. 1-5, points; nos. 6 and 12, oval scrapers; nos. 7-9, scrapers; no. 10, disk; nos. 13-14, bones bearing marks of flint implements through pressure flaking; 1/4 natural size. (Reprinted from G. G. MacCurdy, *Human Origins: A Manual of Prehistory*, 1924, by permission of the Peabody Museum of Archeology, Cambridge, Mass.)

Although this classification of prehistoric technologies was invented to accomodate artifacts found in Europe, it was assumed to be applicable to tool traditions throughout the prehistoric world. Now we know that this idea is unfounded, although for geographical regions immediately adjacent to Europe some of these names are useful in a very general way to describe tool traditions which might bear a relationship to European modes of working stone. Local names for tool traditions have replaced the earlier European terminologies, and the European terminologies themselves have become complex as a consequence of more recent research. However, Mousterian has been retained as an appropriate term for the archeological facies associated with European Neanderthals for a period of some 40,000 years. In a looser sense, Mousterian is applied to related lithic technologies within a broad geographical range extending from western Europe and North Africa to parts of the Near East and as far into Asia as Afghanistan and Soviet central Asia. The Ordos region of Inner Mongolia has yielded stone tools which are called Mousterian by some contemporary prehistorians (Figure 5).

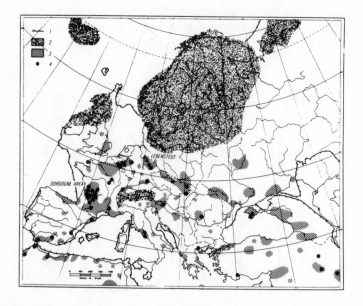

Figure 5. European settlement during the early Würm. (1) Approximate position of the coastlines; (2) glaciers with borders tentatively approximated; (3) distribution of Mousterian and related industries; (4) sites with human skeletal remains dating from the late third interglacial and early Würm. (Reprinted from K. W. Butzer, *Environment and Archaeology,* 1971 by permission of Aldine Publishing Company)

Although tools were not recovered with the human remains from the Neander Valley and Gibraltar, both were found together at Sipka in 1880, at Spy in 1886, at Taubach in 1892-1895, at Ochoz in 1905, at Le Moustier and La Chapelle-aux-Saints in 1908, at La Ferrassie in 1909, and in the Neanderthal sites discovered later in this century. These discoveries have established that tools of the Mousterian flake tradition were manufactured by Neanderthals. However, few prehistorians would go so far as to claim that these are the only products of stone working to be associated with this population. No longer does the term Mousterian cover all of the varied tool industries which have been found at factory, habitation, and surface sites dated to the Middle Paleolithic. Other names had to be coined to include different patterns and methods of stone working. For example, in southern France, Würm I industries are characterized by the presence of utilized flakes struck from discoidal cores, the "typical" Mousterian flaking technique, while in the northern part of France, collateral tool manufacturers were practicing a method whereby flakes were struck from cores which had been initially prepared by a faceting of the core from which the flake was to be struck, a technique called "Levalloisian." Now this latter procedure has an antiquity in the Lower Paleolithic industries of southern Africa, but in many so-called Mousterian sites it makes its appearance alongside the unprepared flake tools of the true Mousterian tradition.

Rather than concluding from this evidence that the different technological traditions were executed by different kinds of hominids, it is more reasonable to assume that we have a broad spectrum of tool forms and techniques produced by a single widely-distributed population adapting to different climates and addressing itself to specific tasks in varied economic pursuits. Local experimentations with tool making would seem probable given the geographic range of Middle Paleolithic settlements across portions of three continents. It seems reasonable to assume that Neanderthals and their collateral kin were the tool makers of Mousterian and Levalloisian products for this vast region rather than some mysterious race about whom we are still ignorant. The phrase "Mousterian Complex" has been adopted to include the technologies of the Middle Paleolithic within the geographical areas considered here.

Some problems arise, however, at the other end of our time scale for Neanderthal man, the era when tools of the Mousterian Complex are replaced by Upper Paleolithic industries and when Neanderthal habitation areas are occupied by men of modern aspect. The makers of the blade tools produced during the later part of the Würm in western Europe just before the flowering of the Aurignacian are known as the "Perigordian I people." They are recognized only by their lithic remains, for no skeletons of this population have been recovered to date. Their tools reflect both Middle and Upper

27

Paleolithic patterns of manufacture, and this industry may indeed be transitional between the two. Deposits of Perigordian tools are dated to 33,000 B.C., and a millenium later this industry was supplanted in some parts of France by the Aurignacian, a fully Upper Paleolithic horizon derived from outside this region, perhaps from eastern Europe and ultimately from Asia. Were the Perigordian I people Neanderthals? Were they the immediate progenitors of the Cro-Magnon, Combe-Capelle, Chancelade, and other Würm III people whom we identify as *Homo sapiens sapiens?* If Neanderthals, had they learned new skills from men of modern aspect prior to their replacement by them? Or, supposing that the Perigordian I people were Neanderthals, had they evolved biologically into *Homo sapiens sapiens* at a time when their technological traditions were also undergoing change? We simply do not know the answers to these questions. Perhaps the study of the physical characteristics of Neanderthal fossils holds a solution to the problem of Neanderthal affinities to the makers of the Upper Paleolithic traditions.

In this chapter we have observed the geological and faunal evidence for dating Neanderthal man *sensu stricto* to the Upper Pleistocene, a time just prior to and during the final glacial advance. We have noted the absence of his fossil remains from deposits associated with the final stadial episode of that final glaciation, Würm III, which suggests that the preceding Würm II-III interstadial marks the time of his disappearance. In Europe the period of Neanderthal occupation may be dated at about 80,000 to 35-40,000 years ago. We have also noted that stone tools of a specific technological tradition called the Mousterian are commonly associated with Neanderthal paleontological data in European sites. Mousterial-like tools occur in North Africa and deep into the heartlands of central Asia. By 33,000 B.C. the European Mousterian (Middle Paleolithic) tool kit is replaced by very different stone-worked artifacts of several Upper Paleolithic traditions. All of these are the products of anatomically modern *Homo sapiens.*

A Neanderthal Prototype

Now let us look at the first detailed study of the bones of Neanderthal man and the influence this description had upon later interpretations of his place in man's evolutionary story. How were Neanderthals understood by anatomists and paleontologists within the paradigm of evolutionary biology?

The finding in 1905 of Mousterian tools at a cave in the commune of La Chapelle-aux-Saints was followed three years later by the excavation of a Neanderthal skeleton at the same site. The cave is in the vicinity of Le Moustier, La Ferrassie, Les Eyzies, and other prehistoric sites in the valley of the Dordogne and its tributaries in southwestern France. The La Chapelle-aux-Saints discovery was remarkable for two reasons. The body had been buried in a ritual position and in association with faunal remains, signs that Neanderthals held some attitudes of respect for their dead. Also, this was the most complete skeleton recovered from western Europe at that time, the postcranial bones from earlier excavated Neanderthal deposits being either absent or fragmentary and few. Nearby, at the cave of Le Moustier, another Neanderthal burial had been found in the year 1908, but the German excavator removed the skeleton to Berlin and collaboration with the French party at La Chapelle-aux-Saints did not take place. Reports of the latter site which were read to the French Academy of Sciences included a summary statement about the skeleton of La Chapelle-aux-Saints. This was prepared by Marcellin Boule, the noted paleontologist at the National Museum of Natural History, Paris. His complete report appeared in a series of long articles in three volumes of the *Annals de Paléontologie* published between 1911 and 1913, by which time the specimen had been cleaned and reconstructed.

Boule's approach to the description of the important skeleton ran along paths well trodden by those scientists of his day who were impressed with the so-called "simian" anatomical features of Neanderthals, and it is in retrospect from our vantage point of having more abundant fossil data and more sophisticated interpretations of human evolution that Boule's conclusions appear so misguided. He fully accepted the fossil evidence as the key to documenting the fact of human evolution, but he did not believe that Neanderthals stood along the phylogenetic stem leading to modern man, the view upheld by others of his colleagues who stressed the importance of certain modern anatomical features of Neanderthal skeletons. Boule rejected any hypothesis that would support the theory of a definite Neanderthal "stage" or "phase" through which sapient man had passed in his evolutionary course towards his present form, and argued that Neanderthals were the withered branch of an evolutionary line coincident with, but independent of, that line leading to man of modern aspect. Our own direct ancestors must be sought elsewhere in the fossil record. Indeed, Boule thought of Neanderthals as representatives of a backward evolutionary group, so impressed was he by this population's primitive anatomical features of low cranial vault height, inclined forehead region, broad nasal structure, and projecting face. Furthermore, if the hypothesis of a Neanderthal stage for the evolutionary pathway leading to modern man was correct, where were the fossils of transitional forms linking *Homo neanderthalensis* to *Homo sapiens*? Such data were not available seventy years ago. Also the apparent suddenness of Neanderthal extinction and termination of the Mousterian tradition seemed to confirm Boule's view that Cro-Magnon man invaded Europe from elsewhere and militantly dispatched the Neanderthal aborigines to early graves. Charged with the task of reconstructing the La Chapelle-aux-Saints specimen, it was understandable that Boule should have given form to these assumptions about Neanderthal man's lowly status.

Less understandable is why the obvious pathological modifications of the skeleton, indicative of arthritis and rickets, were not taken into account more fully. When William L. Straus of Johns Hopkins Medical College and A.J.E. Cave of St. Bartholomew's Hospital Medical College, London, reexamined the La Chapelle-aux-Saints skeleton in Paris in 1955 (at which time they were surprised at the fragmentary nature of the specimen and the consequent extent of restoration required), they found that the vertebrae were severly deformed. Yet Boule had passed over their pathological changes and had attributed the following type of posture to "normal" Neanderthals:

The differences between the skeleton of Neanderthal man and that of modern man are such that they necessarily imply certain differences in the general bearing and attitude of the body. The great development of the face, the backward position of the foramen magnum which must have caused the body to incline forward, the slighter curve of the cervical and lumbar regions of the vertebral column, and the distinctly simian arrangement of the spinous processes of the cervical vertebrae, all testify to this fact. With regard to the lower limb, it is clear that if the formation of the pelvis and the great development of the gluteal muscles indicate that biped attitude had already been attained, the anatomical characters of femur and tibia, seen in profile in the upright position, show that the leg and thigh, when extended, could not have been in a precisely straight line with each other; that the femur must have sloped downwards and forwards, and that the tibia, sloping in a contrary direction, must have formed a wide angle with the femur. So that, without being mechanically impossible, the total extension of the knee could not have been normal, and the habitual attitude must have been one of semi-flexions. The fibula, stronger in character, had a most important part to play as a support. The general appearance of the articulations of the foot indicates a greater degree of mobility and freedom. The foot, still only slightly arched, must have rested on the ground on its outer edge, and must have assumed naturally an in-toed position; the wide separation of the great toe shows that it may have played the part of a prehensile organ. In general, the ordinary normal carriage of Neanderthal man must then have differed in some degree from our own.

Straus and Cave (1957) presented a paper at a 1956 symposium, held to commemorate the centenary of the discovery of the Neander Valley specimen, in which they announced that their study of all of the bones from La Chapelle-aux-Saints provided no support to the assumption that the posture of Neanderthals differed significantly from that of present-day men. However, they did not reject the fact that the skull and postcranial bones of this extinct population did exhibit some features which distinguished it as a group from populations of modern men. While the arthritic "old man" of La Chapelle-aux-Saints may have stood and walked in an abnormal manner, similar locomotor behavior would be expectable in contemporary sufferers of spinal osteoarthritis. In short, the Boulian description of Neanderthal posture and movement pattern is appropriate to pathologically deformed victims of arthritis (and perhaps rickets too), but is in no way applicable to a Neanderthal in sound health (Figure 6).

Boule's description of the intellect of Neanderthals, based upon his study of endocranial casts of his prototypic specimen, is even less flattering than what we have encountered already. He stated that in

the simplicity and coarse appearance of the convolutions ... the brain of Neanderthal man more resembles the brains of the great anthropoid apes or of microcephalic man . . . [with respect to] the relative development of his frontal lobe, which is debased and slants backwards [Neanderthal man] may

31

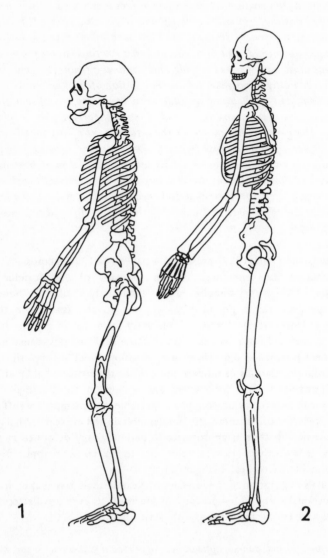

Figure 6. Reconstruction of the posture of Neanderthal man according to (1) Boule and (2) Weinert. Not drawn to scale. (After Boule and Vallois, 1957)

be thus ranked between the anthropoid apes and modern man, and even nearer to the former than to the latter . . . . It is probable, therefore, that Neanderthal man must have possessed only a rudimentary psychic nature, superior certainly to that of the anthropoid apes, but markedly inferior to that of any modern race whatever. He had doubtless only the most rudimentary articulate language. On the whole, the brain of this fossil Man is already a human brain because of the amount of its cerebral matter; but this matter does not yet show the superior organization which characterizes Modern Men.

With regard to the archeological evidence of Neanderthal man's intelligence, Boule makes this judgment:

It is important to note that the physical characters of the Neanderthal type are quite in agreement with what archaeology teaches us as to his bodily capacity, his psychology, and his habits. As we have already pointed out, there is hardly a more rudimentary or degraded form of industry than that of our Mousterian Man. His use of one simple material only, stone—apart probably from wood and bone—the uniformity, simplicity and rudeness of his stone implements, and the probable absence of all traces of any pre-occupation of an aesthetic or of a moral kind, are quite in agreement with the brutish appearance of this energetic and clumsy body, of the heavy-jawed skull, which itself still declares the predominance of functions of a purely vegetative or bestial kind over the functions of the mind . . . . What contrast with the men of the next geological and archaeological period, with the men of the Cro-Magnon type, who had a more elegant body, a finer head, an upright and spacious brow, and who have left, in the caves which they inhabited, so much evidence of their manual skill, artistic and religious preoccupations, of their abstract facilities, and who were the first to merit the glorious title of Homo sapiens!

So fared Neanderthal man at the hands of this learned paleontologist who was more impressed by the low and inclined frontal region of the skull, which he interpreted as indicating rudimentary development of the frontal lobe of the brain once considered to be the seat of intellectual powers, than by the large cranial capacities of Neanderthal skulls. The adaptive effectiveness of the Mousterian technological tradition and the burial customs implying a respect for the dead, if not a sense of affection and sorrow over a personal loss, were other interpretations of the anthropological evidence which Boule overlooked.

Finally we should note that while Boule described his specimen as an "old man" in the sixth decade of life at the time of his demise, more recent investigators have reestimated the age of this male to be just under forty years or perhaps between forty and fifty years. However, an adult of that age might be considered old for a paleolithic population.

Today we can understand why Boule found it expedient to turn to the Neanderthal specimens already known in his day from the Neander Valley, Spy, La Ferrassie, and other sites in order to fill in the gaps of the skeletal data from La Chapelle-aux-Saints, for the latter were not as complete as the broad sweep of Boulian interpretations would imply. However, the French paleontologist did not treat the skeleton he described as a single individual in a population composed of other persons demonstrating a normal range of anatomical variations, as one finds in any biotic group, ancient or modern. Instead he attempted to define a "prototype," a model with which other fossil specimens were to be compared in any assessment of their taxonomic status. This exemplifies one of the important changes in evolutionary biology which has occurred since the time that Boule wrote his reports, the shift from *typological* thinking to *populational* thinking in seeking to understand biological variation and change over time and space.

The weight of Boule's authority as a scholar influenced many of his colleagues working well outside the portals of the National Museum of Natural History in Paris to carry out their own studies of fossil man using as a model Boule's definitive study of the La Chapelle-aux-Saints skeleton. Grafton Elliot Smith (1924), a professor of anatomy at University College in London, wrote of Neanderthal man:

His short, thick-set, and coarsely built body was carried in a half-stooping slouch upon short, powerful, and half-flexed legs of peculiarly ungraceful form. His thick neck sloped forward from the broad shoulders to support the massive flattened head, which protruded forward, so as to form an unbroken curve of neck and back, in place of the alternation of curves which is one of the graces of the truly erect Homo sapiens. The heavy, overhanging eyebrow-ridges and retreating forehead, the great coarse face with its large eye-sockets, broad nose, and receding chin, combined to complete the picture of unattractiveness, which it is more probably than not was still further emphasized by a shaggy covering of hair over most of the body. The arms were relatively short, and the exceptionally large hands lacked the delicacy and nicely balanced co-operation of thumb and fingers which is regarded as one of the most distinctive of human characteristics.

Even as late as the 1950s these notions of Neanderthal man persisted in anthropological literature, particularly with respect to the question of his possession of a completely upright gait. But a few scientists such as Gustav Schwalbe (1923) in Alsatian Germany, Arthur Keith (1925) and W. E. Le

Gros Clark (1955) in England, and Ernest Hooton (1946) in the United States, were anticipating the researches of Straus and Cave in offering revisions of Boule's reconstruction. In fact at the time Straus and Cave were in Paris, the French anthropologists Camille Arambourg (1955) and Étienne Patte (1955) were seeing through the press their respective publications which contained conclusions reached independently, but paralleling to a remarkable degree those of Straus and Cave. Today it is in the popular literary and graphic media where Boulian Neanderthals continue to slouch about with bent knees and idiotic faces, subhuman brutes forcibly escorting by the hair prospective mates into their dens. Several of our well-known museums of natural history, both in the United States and abroad, have yet to remove their panoramic murals and plaster models of apish Neanderthals at work and play, and only lately have these characterizations left the pages of popular books purporting to be about anthropology.

It should be clear from the survey of historical events outlined in this chapter why "cave men" in general and Neanderthal man in particular have been depicted in these inaccurate representations over so many years. With respect to our present understanding of Neanderthal man, the past twenty years have seen the emergence of very different points of view from those just described concerning his skeletal anatomy and behavior. It is to these current interpretations that we now turn.

Skeletal Anatomy of Western European Neanderthals

One of the most conspicuous features of modern evolutionary biology is the abandonment of the venerable practice of defining type patterns for species and subspecies whereby a particular specimen would be selected from a group to be held up as the archetype to which all other individuals in real or presumed relationship to it might be compared. For centuries this was a perfectly respectable objective of naturalists seeking to classify biotic phenomena. The historic roots of the concept are traceable to Plato who saw the cosmos composed of a real world of Ideas, the realm of the Divine Mind, and the illusory world which man perceives by his senses. With the ferment of interest in newly-discovered lands and their exotic, unfamiliar living things, many scholars of the Renaissance and Enlightenment assumed the pious task of classifying the products of the Creator's efforts. Beginning with a study of minerals, simple life forms, and plants, on through the overwhelming complexities of higher animals, these classifiers of nature went on to the grouping of mankind into discrete races below the species level. Philosophers continued this hierarchy of nature into the realm of the supernatural, ordering and describing the roles of angels and intermediate forms until the Absolute Being was attained. By so defining the idealized form of all existing phenomena, the naturalist-philosopher saw himself recognizing the blueprint of the world; his typological identifications were in essence the Ideas in the mind of the Creator.

This was the tradition in which Linnaeus and his students carried out their collection and classifying. We have noted already that this was nonevolutionary in scope since the kinds of living things classified were held to be immutable. Preoccupation with defining types of living things precluded consideration of the concept that normal variation between individuals of a group could be thought to be of any importance. Variants of a population were dismissed as the irrelevant departures from the idealized form, the products of chance environmental influences which tended to obscure the true identity of a group of related organisms. Only the most discerning and experienced taxonomist examining a collection of specimens on his· work table could reach the proper decision as to which anatomical characters were fundamental to the group and which were aberrant, i.e., variable.

These ancient tenets were threatened by the ascendancy of Darwinian evolutionary theory, for Darwin rejected the abstraction of the archetype and regarded the variants of a population as the building blocks of new species by the operation of the process he called natural selection. But it was with the emergence of genetics at the turn of this century as a scientific discipline investigating the laws of inheritance, and the gradual assimilation of genetic theory with evolutionary biology that biologists came to appreciate the opportunities implicit in a population approach. This is the orientation of modern biological researchers, whether they are students of virus colonies or of fossil and living men. We are much more sensitive now to the complex affinities of populations to ecosystems than were biologists of even a few years ago.

While contemporary paleontologists are fully in agreement with these recent shifts in biological orientations, and have made significant contributions to the new biology, the nature of fossil data presents them with some special problems which are not shared in quite the same way by their colleagues working with living populations. Complete skeletons of the larger extinct creatures are not always preserved in the earth. Even with the good fortune of finding a number of fossil specimens in a single locality, the question of the degree of contemporaneity must be raised, and for specimens with similar anatomical characters collected over a wide geographical range, the assignment of these to a single "population" can be made only in a very general way. Some extinct groups of animals are recognized only through the accident of discovery by single parts of their skeletal anatomy, structures such as skulls and teeth. Reconstruction of entire organisms may remain tentative until more complete skeletal remains are located and correctly associated with fossil fragments already collected. Soft-part anatomy, namely integument, ears, noses, etc. are very seldom preserved. Pigmentation features are usually nonrecoverable. Sex and age (at time of death) determinations depend upon the survival of particular bones which bear recognizable secondary sexual features and growth markers. These, and a variety of other problems, force the student of the fossil record to be extremely careful in describing the normal range of anatomical and behavioral variation for a group of ancient organisms, even when a large series of related specimens is available for analysis. But until the paleontologist has some firm impression of these degrees of differences, he cannot be confident that his taxonomic allocations are reasonable. This is not to say that the task of the systematist examining living organisms is without its complications too, but if we continue to use reproductive isolation as an operative criterion for the identification of species, it is obvious that the kinds of observations made in the field and laboratory by paleontological researchers are of a different order of magnitude.

These considerations are prefatory to our understanding of the skeletal biology and adaptive variability of Neanderthal man. Although we are blessed, after a century and a quarter of fruitful discovery, with sufficient bones of Neanderthals to fill a churchyard of modest size (and may even observe some fossil impressions of Neanderthal footprints in some Italian caves), we must bear in mind that we are considering a group of ancient men who were adapted to a variety of econiches extending from Spain to Soviet central Asia. Are we justified in christening all of these fossils by the collective term "Neanderthal"? Some anthropologists have said yes; others strongly disagree. Perhaps we can better appreciate the issues of this ongoing controversy when we discuss the problems of Neanderthal man's ancestors and the puzzle of his extinction. For the moment, let us turn to a description of those western European people of the early and middle Würm, the manufacturers of the Mousterian tools, whom all anthropologists agree deserve the honorific of Neanderthal and for whom general consensus exists as to the uniqueness of certain features of their skeletal anatomy. The adaptive significance of some of these anatomical variables is a subject of debate in anthropology today, but no one would ascribe these to pathologies as some earlier scholars had thought (Bilsborough 1972).

We have observed that the posture and locomotor pattern of Neanderthal man are not significantly different from that which we find in man today, although particular portions of Neanderthal postcranial anatomy do show some distinguishing characteristics which allow us to recognize his bones in deposits where he lies buried. For example, his massive thigh bone (femur) exhibits a slight to pronounced degree of curvature along the length of the shaft, and the proximal end of the lower leg bone (tibia) is often retroflexed. Both of these features do appear, however, within the normal range of anatomical variation of modern man. It has been suggested by some osteologists that the retroflexed tibial head is a structural correlate of the practice of frequent bending of the knee. This does appear in rather high frequencies among contemporary mountain-dwelling people as well as among those persons whose habitual resting posture is a squat. That this may have been a preferred resting posture of Neanderthals is indicated by the morphology of the tibia and by the presence of supernumerary articular facets, the so-called squatting facets on the distal ends of the tibiae and on the talus bones of the feet. These are other features found on the limb bones of squatters. When standing erect, Neanderthals were as efficient as we are in extending and locking the knee. Their bodies did not have a significantly different center of gravity from that of man today, and they certainly did not stand in a posture of habitual genuflexion nor risk a sprained neck whenever looking upward to the sky, as Boule and others would have had us believe!

The bones of the upper extremities and the pectoral girdle show some interesting features which again are shared in varying degrees and frequencies by modern man. The collar bone (clavical) has large articular extremities. The shoulder blade (scapula) is more sharply inclined upwards than is usual in modern human populations. The muscular attachments of the upper arm bone (humerus) and lower arm bones (radius and ulna) are robust, with the radial and ulnar shafts exhibiting some bowing. As with the clavical, the articular ends of these long bones are quite large.

Neanderthal handbones are robust, too. A recent survey of skeletal remains of the Neanderthal hand by J. Musgrave (1971) describes it as having a long palm with large-headed metacarpals and digits which have relatively short first joints and long distal joints. These features define a hand with a capacity for a broad span and a powerful grasp. The opposability of the thumb and index finger seems to have been particularly well adapted to a "key grip" type of prehension. A "tip-to-tip" type of opposition of these two digits seems to have been less effective. The significance of these features is uncertain at present, but we should not be justified in concluding that these are primitive or simian traits. The level of technological skill demanded to produce the Mousterian tool industry is sufficient proof that the hands of its manufacturers were not too unlike our own.

From these data of the postcranial skeleton of the western European Neanderthals, we perceive a body build that was short, stocky, and muscular. Stature may have been just over five feet for males whose average weight has been estimated at about 160 pounds. The extremities of the body were short and trunks were relatively long and heavy. The thorax was full. This type of body form reflects some of the anatomical features characteristic of cold-adapted populations living today, perhaps not so surprising a parallel if we consider the climatic conditions of a glacial environment prevailing in Europe during much of the time of Neanderthal man's habitation there. When we look at some of the anatomical features of the Neanderthal skull, certain structures related to cold adaptation seem to be present. It is interesting that as we move eastward and southward from the glaciated and tundra-forest ecological settings and look at other fossil series from populations living at the same period of time, we find that the extreme anatomical expressions of cold adaptation begin to disappear. Such characters are much less obvious or even nonexistent among those Neanderthal collaterals inhabiting warmer climatic zones of Asia and North Africa.

Some authors, aware of the high incidence of arthritic markers in Neanderthal skeletal anatomy, have suggested that Neanderthal adaptation to cold stress was far from being completely effective. Perhaps the arthritic factor present in so many skeletal remains is indicative of an even higher incidence of respiratory diseases which may have led to the eventual extinction of the population. The presence of rickets, diagnosed by the extreme bowing of the long bones of some specimens, has been interpreted to mean that Neanderthals had little access to dietary vitamin D because of a climatic screening of ultraviolet radiation during periods of glacial optima when snow and sleet were year-round phenomena. Certainly the question of an insufficiently balanced diet must be raised in this connection too. If flesh foods provided the bulk of the diet, as they do among many contemporary hunting-gathering populations, essential vitamins and minerals may be absent. Only a more exhaustive study of the Neanderthal skeleton can support or reject these hypotheses of climatic adaptation and the effects of disease. The issue here is not whether cold adaptation and resistence to the disabling affects of certain diseases were important factors in the lifeways of Neanderthals, but rather to what degree are these environmental pressures properly interpreted in our study of the osteological remains.

The capacity values of the brain-bearing portion of the cranial vault of Neanderthals provides ranges of 1525 to 1640 cc. (cubic centimeters) for males and 1300 to 1425 cc. for females, both from very small series. Studies of Neanderthals which include some of the western Asiatic collaterals with the ranges and means of western European Neanderthals show a range of 1270 to 1795 cc. and a mean of 1550 cc. Other estimates using skulls of both sexes from western European specimens show a range of 1145 to 1795 cc. with a mean of 1470 cc. The mean value of cranial capacities of modern man is 1370 cc. including males and females. Female capacity values are lower by as much as 175 cc. when compared with values for males in populations of *Homo sapiens sapiens*. As we see, the cranial capacities of Neanderthals are slightly higher than for contemporary human beings. Brain size alone is not an index of intelligence, and "normal" cranial capacities for individuals in modern populations have the broad range of from 950 to 2200 cc. Capacities on either side of these limits usually indicate neurological pathologies of various kinds. What is most striking about the high values of Neanderthal cranial capacities is that these are not encountered in skulls of earlier prehistoric people, although some of the lower values for Neanderthals turn up at the upper end of the range of values among their predecessors.

The shape of the Neanderthal cranial vault is different from that of earlier and later populations, too. The anterior portion of the brain is flatter and longer than that of modern man's brain, while the posterior portion is broader. This shape factor is reflected in the morphology of the long Neanderthal skull itself with its low forehead, bulging sides, and protuberant occipital bone, the so-called "chignon" or bun at the back of the skull. The brow ridges are heavy and fairly even in size across the frontal bone, arching above each orbit in a way not encountered in earlier skulls. The sinuses are concentrated in the medial portion of the torus but do not extend above the brow ridge itself and into the forehead region as these frontal air sacs may do in skulls of modern man. Thoroughly modern is the anterior position of the foramen magnum, the large aperture at the base of the skull through which the spinal cord passes to the brain. This is another indication that Neanderthals walked erect, their heads nicely balanced above the vertebral column. The occipital torus marking the attachments of the neck muscles is situated well below the back of the head and without any pronounced angulation as is seen in pre-Mousterian fossil men. That is, the pattern of the nuchal area is within the range of morphological variation of man today. The mastoid processes are smaller than those seen in contemporary human populations (Figure 7).

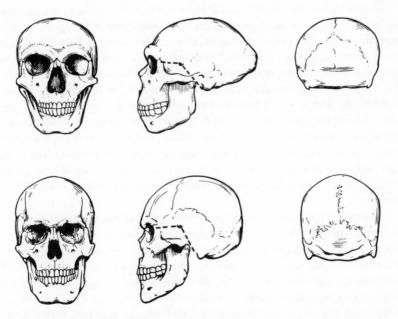

Figure 7. Comparison of skulls of Neanderthal man (upper row) and modern man (lower row). (From *Mankind in the Making*, copyright © 1959, 1967 by William Howells. Reprinted by permission of Doubleday & Co., Inc.)

Neanderthal skulls are especially distinctive from both earlier and later men with respect to facial architecture. The middle portion of the face is extraordinarily long and projects from the area of the lower margins of the orbits to the tooth-bearing parts of the upper jaw. One is struck immediately by the appearance of the anterior orientation of the teeth relative to the bony parts of the jaws. This feature is especially obvious in the positioning of the molar teeth in the mandible where the third molar is usually situated well forward of the margin of the ascending part of the jaw (ramus), when viewed from the side. In other mandibles from earlier prehistoric or contemporary series this molar is partially obscured by the ramus. Examination of the nasal bones and periform aperture of the nasal chamber reveals that the nose was prominent and broad. The cheek bones (malars) slope posteriorly towards the ear and do not form the same kind of angulation that appears in the less prominent faces of modern crania. From a visual inspection of the side of the skull, one notes a greater expanse of orbital surface than is the case with many other non-Neanderthal specimens, while a frontal view of the skull shows the rounded shape of the orbits. These variables are correlated with the height of the face and its prominence. The distance between the orbits is greater than it is in most modern skulls.

Other anatomical variables of the Neanderthal face may be noted, such as the absence of a canine depression on the maxilla, the convergence of the maxillary walls, a peculiar articulation of the tempero-mandibular joint, and some anomalies of the ear region. The mandible is not especially large, and its lack of a chin has been interpreted as a product of the forward placement of the entire dentition relative to both the rest of the jaw and the upper face. Structurally, a chin would have been present had the face been retracted; the lower part of the mandible has a length within the size range for modern man. Teeth are close in size to those of man today, but the incisors are somewhat thicker in the lingual-labial direction, especially along the gum line. The roots and pulp cavities of Neanderthal molars are large, a condition called "taurodonty." This is found in moderate frequency in some existing human groups.

Several explanations have been advanced to explain the adaptive significance of this type of facial architecture. Carleton Coon (1962), an anthropologist formerly at the University of Pennsylvania and author of a provocative book on the origin of human racial groups, has favored the view that the prognathic, large-nosed structures of the Neanderthal face were adaptive responses to thermal pressures of the glacial environment, as were some of the postcranial features of the Neanderthal skeleton, as discussed below. Coon argued that a large nose had the advantage of warming inhaled air, thus protecting the lungs from cold as the air passed through the passage of mucous membrane. The increase in the size of the facial sinuses and the large malars, which are structurally correlated with the evolution of a prominent nose, served to insulate still further the exposed face and nasal passage. At the same time these structures afforded greater protection to the arteries carrying blood to the temperature-sensitive brain. Some recent tests for cold adaptability conducted by A.T. Steegman, Jr. (1972), using students of Japanese and northern European descent, do suggest a greater degree of cold tolerance among those subjects with long, projecting faces and nonprojecting malars. Persons with relatively slanted vaults also maintained a more even skin temperature, this measure rather than physical discomfort being the criterion of cold adaptability.

The anthropologist F. Clark Howell (1952, 1957) of the University of California, Berkeley, had earlier suggested that Neanderthal populations had been geographically isolated for varying periods of time when ice sheets in northern and highland Europe and stretches of inhospitable tundra rendered communication infeasible with other human groups of that period. He surmised that genetic drift and/or the operation of natural selection on this isolated Neanderthal population of western Europe might account for the physical characteristics which distinguish these ancient people from their relatives in eastern Europe and western Asia. Perhaps the opinions of both Coon (1962) and Howell (1952) are helpful to us in understanding why Neanderthal body form and cranial architecture are confined to a specific part of the world during early to middle Würm times. Of course the evolution of these features may have arisen before the onset of the Würm glaciation among the ancestors of western European Neanderthals living during the previous glacial period. Fossil remains of the men of the Riss are not yet sufficiently abundant to either confirm or reject this hypothesis.

While not offered as a counter to these interpretations of thermal adaptation, two other American anthropologists, D. S. Brose and M. H. Wolpoff (1971), have asked whether the thick incisor teeth and forward orientation of all of the teeth of the Neanderthal dentition might not be explicable in terms of the mouth having been used for grasping purposes, i.e., as a gripping device with selective pressures favoring large anterior teeth, massive roots, and stout alveolar sockets. These traits would maximize the effectiveness of a prominent mouth with powerful gripping functions. There is sufficient documentation in the ethnographic record of a wide range of uses in which contemporary people have used their teeth, as in chewing leather to soften it for clothing, straightening wooden arrow shafts, stripping vines, husking fruit, and even prying off Coke bottle tops! However, W. W. Howells (1973a, 1973b, 1974) of Harvard University, who has done so much to advance research on Neanderthal man through a multivariate-analysis approach, would regard the dental specializations as structural correlates of evolutionary changes of the upper facial region of Neanderthals. Howells notes that their highly specialized faces are not encountered in high frequency among other populations where the evidence for vigorous dental prehension is documented.

Howells has been able to demonstrate the unique features of the Neanderthal face and dentition by turning away from the traditional practice of simply comparing a limited number of separate anatomical characters and facing instead the implications revealed in a study of the "total morphological pattern" of a population. This term he borrows from the work of the British anatomist W. E. Le Gros Clark (1955) who had discussed the configuration of anatomical traits distinguishing groups of organisms from one another. By comparing Neanderthal and modern crania using ten multiple discriminant functions that express patterns of shape, rather than size or the effects of single measurements, Howells shows that the Neanderthal skulls from La Chapelle-aux-Saints and La Ferrassie score beyond the individual limits of any of seventeen populations in a sample of eight hundred skulls. Only skulls of anatomically modern *Homo sapiens* fall within the distribution of modern mean scores. It would be difficult to argue that Neanderthals are really morphologically transitional between Middle Pleistocene men and modern Europeans on the basis of Howell's statistical data.

In this chapter we have reviewed the major features of the skeletal anatomy of Neanderthal man of Western Europe. In some characters this Upper Pleistocene hominid is unique, but other structural features are not significantly different from those the anthropologist encounters in world populations today. The issues which are most important to contemporary students of Neanderthal man have to do with the interpretations of the fossil hominid's physiological adaptation to the cold stresses of his glacial environment as these adaptations are reflected in skeletal traits. It is in the morphology of the Neanderthal skull and especially of the face that the most obvious features of Neanderthal man's uniqueness are encountered.

Some Neanderthal
Collaterals

Having become familiar with the anatomical variables of the Neanderthal skeleton and some of the hypotheses which have been offered to explain the adaptive significance of its distinctive features, we are better prepared now to understand the relationships of the Neanderthals of western Europe to those populations contemporary with them in time, but inhabiting lands outside their geographical range of activity. In the discussion which follows we should keep in mind the question of whether all of these collateral populations should be recognized as Neanderthals or whether some should be excluded from this category of Neanderthals *sensu stricto* on the basis of their anatomical differences. In this chapter we shall review the record of fossil finds of the Upper Pleistocene in eastern Europe, Asia, and Africa.

Eastern Europe may have been even colder than the western lands during periods of glacial optima, but proof of its occupation by man during the Würm is found in the skeletal remains and associated Mousterian artifacts derived from caves and open-air deposits of windborne dust (loess) laid down on the plains. We mentioned earlier the importance of the discovery in 1880 of a child's mandible at the cave of Šipka in Czechoslovakia. This was one of those fossil specimens which Virchow had dismissed as merely another overrated find of a pathologically deformed individual of recent history. Czechoslovakian anthropologists have been very active in fossil research during the past few decades, and Jan Jelinek (1969), Director of the Moravian Museum at Brno, with his associates has dated the occupation of Šipka to the time of the Würm I-II interstadial (Göttweig).* Furthermore, they have noted

---

*Recently European archaeologists have determined that the Göttweig-type site material is actually Riss-Würm. Other material called Göttweig comes from more than one Würm interstadial.

that at the time the Šipka site was occupied by makers of Mousterian tools, a community of indisputable *Homo sapiens sapiens* people was coexistent in the nearby Mladec caves in this same mountain region to the north of the Morava River. Their tools were not of the Mousterian tradition, but were more like industries associated with later Würm peoples of western Europe. Was the Šipka skeleton that of a Neanderthal? Were two different kinds of men living side-by-side in this part of eastern Europe during the Göttweig?

An examination of the mandible from Šipka might provide some answers. The jaw is massive and contains large teeth, traits we have seen in high frequency among western European Neanderthals. But the latter are essentially chinless, and the Šipka mandible supports a chin, a feature of modern-type man. Between the tooth-bearing portion of the mandible and the chin is a horizontal depression called the "subalveolar incisure," a concomitant of chin development in *Homo sapiens sapiens*. Admittedly there are difficulties in comparing the bones of children to adults, and the Šipka specimen is that of a preadolescent. Variations attributed to sexual dimorphism cannot be clearly defined and the bones, being smaller, are less likely to be in as good a state of preservation as bones of the mature skeleton. The relative paucity of comparative material from infants, children, and adolescents intensifies the problems of the student of comparative osteology. However, for Neanderthal and collateral populations, relatively good preadult skeletal series exist. As we know more about these skeletons, we stand a better chance of responding to the kind of question posed at Šipka.

The Ochoz cave has been excavated several times beginning in 1905 and more recently between 1953 and 1955. In association with Mousterian tools, an incomplete massive jaw was found, one of the largest jaws on record for Neanderthals, if we can include it in this population. The overall height of the mandible is very impressive, and the incisor teeth exhibit a marked degree of alveolar projection. This feature sets another record in Neanderthal mandibular finds. It comes close to the Spy 1 Neanderthal specimen in the great length of the molar row. Taurodonty is present of which the third molar is especially large. There is an obvious space between the distal border of the third molar and the region of the mandible where the ramus begins its ascent. All of these features would qualify the Ochoz mandible to membership in the Neanderthal club. But some modern features are present, too. Below the subalveolar incisure is a distinct chin. While not projecting, indeed of a chin form called "negative," it is nevertheless a feature found more often in the mandibles of modern-type men than in Neanderthals *sensu stricto*. While originally dated to the third interglacial period, Ochoz would now seem to be later, at least Würm I in date.

Two other sites in eastern Europe have been excavated more recently. Kůlna cave in the western sector of Czechoslovakia was dug in 1965, and four years earlier the gravels of the Váh River near the town of Šala in the central part of the country were recognized as a fossil deposit. Kůlna has been dated as contemporary with Šipka. The right portion of an upper jaw with some teeth in place was found here in association with Mousterian tools. The eruption and wear patterns of the teeth indicate that the specimen was a juvenile of about fifteen years of age. The height of the maxilla is striking and within the range of variation for western European Neanderthals. However, the presence of a weak canine fossa is not a characteristic of the latter population. The Šala discovery is also of a young person, perhaps a young adult female. The evidence is limited to a frontal bone found without associated remains of faunal material or artifacts, but in all probability it can be related to a nearby bone bed of later third interglacial or early Würm I fauna. The bone has a higher forehead region than is typical of the Neanderthals we have been describing, but the pronounced development of the supraorbital torus (brow ridges), rounded upper orbital margins, and broad nasal root are traits with which we are already familiar from our description of the Šala lady's western neighbors.

This list does not exhaust the number of prehistoric human remains found in eastern Europe, for this part of the continent has yielded many excellent sites with the bones of modern-type man, specimens we would assign immediately to *Homo sapiens sapiens* on the basis of their skeletal anatomy as well as because of their archaeological associations. These are the people of the late Würm and subsequent times. Even more exciting to the student of Neanderthal man is the fact that these countries also contain the remains of men of modern anatomical aspect in some deposits of third interglacial date! We shall return to this matter when we have completed the survey of Neanderthal collaterals who were living during the early and middle parts of the final glaciation.

The quest for early man in the Near East began at the turn of the century with the discovery of a supposed Neanderthal fetus in the Grotte d'Antelias in Lebanon, although a catalog of Stone Age artifacts had been made in 1878 listing artifacts collected forty years earlier. In 1925 the Israel cave of Mugharet el-Zuttiyeh near the Sea of Galilee, with its famous "Galilee skull" dating to 70,000 years ago, was explored. Three years later the Shukba cave near Jerusalem, dating to 35,000 years ago, yielded the bones of adult individuals who were identified by their describers as Neanderthals, largely on the basis of their association with early and middle Würm fauna and Mousterian-related tool industries. It was with the excavations at the caves of Mugharet et-Tabun and Mugharet es-Skhūl between 1929 and 1934 that the model designed to describe prehistoric events in Europe was recognized as being inapplicable to other parts of the world. No longer could the equation of "Würm I = Mousterian = Neanderthal man" be applied uncritically to areas outside of Germany, Belgium, Spain, and France.

The two caves of Tabun and Skhūl are situated in the Mount Carmel range near the port of Haifa. Their occupation period extends in time from late Acheulian levels of the end of the third interglacial through the early and middle Würm where handaxes are replaced by Levalloiso-Mousterian flake tools. In the Tabun cave the skeleton of a female and the mandible of a male were found. Skeletons of some eleven individuals were procured from the neighboring Skhūl cave of which four were either remains of infants or incomplete portions of adults. At the time of their discovery, it seemed probable that the two caves had been occupied simultaneously, but more recent dating analysis, using amino acid racemization on bone tissue from human skeletons and comparative faunal analysis, strongly suggests that Tabun was occupied several thousand years earlier than Skhūl. The latter has been dated to about 36,000 years ago.

The mandible of the Tabun male reminds one of the Ochoz jaw in its massiveness and its long dental row. The mandible associated with the Tabun female skeleton is also quite large and, like Neanderthal jaws, is without a chin. While her skull is robust, she lacks the occipital bun so common to Würm I-II populations in western Europe. Her cranial capacity of 1270 cc. is also rather lower than one finds for Neanderthal females. But on the whole, we cannot fail to recognize a morphological similarity to those skeletal remains labeled Neanderthal when found in Europe.

Analysis of the skeletal contents of the Skhūl cave presents a more uncertain picture of Neanderthal affinities. While skull numbers 2, 4, 7, and 9 resemble Neanderthals in many of their features, skulls 5 and 6 share many of their anatomical variables with modern-type man. Let us look at the specimen Skhūl 5, one of the best-preserved of the series. This is an adult male with a brain case of modern form, reduced frontal sinuses within the projecting brows, large mastoid processes, and a well-formed chin on the moderately large mandible. The cranial capacity is estimated as 1518 cc. These features, plus the fact that the limb bones are straight and relatively gracile, depict an individual with many of the anatomical features diagnostic of modern men. Yet this same specimen retains Neanderthal features of large teeth which are placed well forward in the dental row. The face is not as projecting as it is in some European Neanderthals.

The Mount Carmel skeletons were described by Arthur Keith, of the Royal College of Surgeons in London, and Theodore D. McCown, then a graduate student and later a professor at the University of California at Berkeley. They proposed some hypotheses to account for this apparent co-existence of Neanderthal man and human beings of modern form within the same area (McCown and Keith 1939, Figure 8). Their work focused on the

Figure 8. Theodore D. McCown (1908-1969) and Sir Arthur Keith (1866-1954). This picture, made in the mid-1930s, shows the young anthropologist and the older anatomist at the time of their preparation and description of the fossil hominids from Skhul and Tabun in Israel. In their book, *The Stone Age of Mount Carmel* (1939), these scholars raised important questions about the biological affinity of Neanderthal man to mankind today. Their cooperative endeavors resulted in one of the most detailed and elegant descriptions of a fossil hominid group ever published. (Courtesy of Mrs. Elizabeth McCown)

following questions: were these two distinct prehistoric populations, interbreeding and forming a new and hybrid population?—or was this a single group in the throes of evolutionary change towards modern man? Their 1939 report was one of the most thorough anatomical studies ever published on a fossil human population: *The Stone Age of Mount Carmel: the Fossil Human*

49

Remains from the Levalloiso-Mousterian. The junior author tended to favor the interpretation that the physical variables observed within the Tabun and Skhūl series more probably represented a normal range of variation for a number of traits present in an essentially contemporary population. Le Gros Clark (1955) complements this interpretation with the statement that the Mount Carmel people represent a transitional population derived from earlier *Homo* enclaves and evolving into *Homo sapiens* of modern form. Howells (1974) has called the ancient Carmelites archaic moderns with some discrete Neanderthal traits marking their earlier line of descent. Even if the recent dating evidence proves beyond the shadow of a doubt that the Tabun occupation was earlier than the habitation of the Skhūl cave, the matter of Tabun men being directly ancestral to Skhūl men remains unresolved. What is most important about the evidence from Mount Carmel is its demonstration that men very similar in some features of their skeletal anatomy to western European Neanderthals were intrinsic elements of those very populations which we can only regard as much nearer in their biological affinity to ourselves. This situation has not been encountered in western Europe for the period of the last glacial optima.

Two other sites in Israel present this problem of Neanderthal-modern *sapiens* affinities in a different light. Near Lake Tiberius is the Amud cave where the bones of five persons in a Mousterian complex were found in 1961. The excavation of the site and the description of its contents was carried out by a team of Japanese anthropologists whose publication, *The Amud Man and His Cave Site* (Suzuki and Takai 1970), is an elegant new classic in the field. One male skeleton described here is that of an individual whose stature in life was well over 170 cm., tall for a Neanderthal. Although the skull is robust, occipital bunning is not present. Mastoid processes are quite large. The cranial capacity sets a record for men of the Würm I period at 1740 cc. Here, as at Mount Carmel, we see an individual with anatomical features similar on the one hand to Neanderthals of western Europe, on the other hand to men of modern aspect. The definite shape of Amud man's pubic bones is different from that of both groups, and is a pelvic feature which turns up among the skeletons of Shanidar cave in northern Iraq. Pelvic anomalies appear in the Skhūl population, too.

Contemporary with Amud man were the prehistoric people of Jebel Qafza in the vicinity of Nazareth. In the early 1930s, fossil hunting brought anthropologists to this cave which subsequent excavation revealed as a mortuary site containing thirteen or more individuals. Cultural associations are Levalloiso-Mousterian. All of the skeletal specimens which have been described thus far show a preponderance of modern anatomical traits. The best-preserved skull is that of a male called Qafza 6. His supraorbital tori are the largest in the series and within them are massive sinuses. His forehead is elevated in a form commonly found in modern man. Although the occipital torus is marked, the profile of the back of the head is modern in form, too. The nonprojecting face exhibits canine fossae. Orbits are low and rectangular. Malars form an angular pattern as in man today. Teeth are only moderately large. The mandible is modern in many of its features of size and shape and it supports a chin. Other skulls from Qafza such as numbers 2, 7, 8, and 9, have even more highly elevated vaults and they are less prognathic. Howells (1974) has not hesitated to call this population an anatomically modern *Homo sapiens* even though it is associated with a Mousterian industry and dates to the Würm I stadial. In many respects its skeletal features are more like those of the prehistoric people of the Skhūl cave than with the specimens from Tabun and Amud, the latter two groups sharing higher frequencies of Neanderthal features, using the western European Neanderthals as a basis for comparison.

Near Beirut, Lebanon, is the rock shelter of Ksar 'Akil from which a skeleton of a seven-year-old child was removed by two American Jesuit priests some forty years ago. Christened "Egbert" by Father Ewing, who reconstructed the skeleton, it has the appearance of a modern-type preadolescent individual. Brow ridges are lacking, contrary to what has been found among some Neanderthal children of about seven years of age. The forehead is vertical, the face is straight in profile (orthognathous), and there is a well-marked chin on the mandible. The latter feature is absent among many Neanderthal child specimens. The associations of the skeleton with a Mousterian tool tradition and faunal assemblages dating to 43,750 years ago, according to one radiocarbon analysis, add to the evidence that modern-type hominids were in the Near East as collaterals of western European Neanderthals. The Turkish sites of Karain near Adala, excavated in 1949, and Musa Dagh have yielded teeth which may be dated to Würm I times, but this remains uncertain for lack of better dating evidence. There were no tool industries directly associated with the teeth in these Turkish sites.

When we move further eastward into Iraq and Iran, and enter central Asia into Uzbekistan and Crimea, even to the borders of India in eastern Afghanistan, the men of the early Würm are found to share a higher frequency of anatomical features with the Near Eastern people of Tabun and Amud and the western European Neanderthals than they do with the men of modern aspect whom we have encountered in eastern Europe and in the lands of Israel and Lebanon. The tool tradition found with the central Asiatic people of this period represents the eastern limit of the Mousterian, and even in local areas of the Ordos region of China, Mousterian-derived stone industries are known.

One of the most remarkable discoveries of these Asiatic people was made at Shanidar cave in the Zagros Mountains of northern Iraq. Work has been conducted there since 1953 under the direction of Ralph Solecki of Columbia University and by T. Dale Stewart of the Smithsonian Institution. They found that the cave had been occupied almost continuously since early Würm times, and in more recent periods Kurdish people had taken advantage of the shelter. The Mousterian deposits were occupied for periods of as long as 46,000 to 60,000 years, although there may have been a temporary abandonment of the cavern during the peak of the first stadial of the Würm. Of the seven well-preserved skeletons from the cave, of which one was an infant and three have been defined as males, all have cranial forms that are rounder than those found among western European Neanderthals. However, in other respects, they resemble them as well as they do the specimens from Tabun and Amud. Many reveal pelvic anomalies, such as we have noted already for specimens from the Near East. The skeleton called Shanidar 1 is remarkable for its large cranial capacity of some 1700 cc., the successful healing of an amputated right arm, and this individual's recovery from trauma to his left eye, a blow which may have rendered him blind. Even a healed bone lesion on his right parietal bone did not shorten his life. Shanidar 4 was buried in high estate, for botanical evidence suggests that this boy's body was placed on a bier of woody branches, hollyhocks, and wild flowers on some sad spring day between 50,000 and 60,000 years ago. This unusual case of interment has led Solecki (1971) to entitle his popular book about the cave *Shanidar: the First Flower People.*

Iran has provided us with some human skeletal remains from two cave sites of the early Würm, the Kermanshah cave near Bisitun and the Tamtama cave near Rezauyeh. Excavations began in 1949 at both places, but the skeletal material has not been thoroughly described as yet. Fossils called Neanderthals by some Soviet anthropologists have been recovered since 1924 at the cave of Kiik-Koba in the Crimea. Two skeletons, both missing skulls, appear to have been true burials. They are deposited in Würm I levels. At another Crimean site called Starosel'e, excavated in 1952, fossil remains of an eighteen-month-old infant have been dated to 35,000 years ago. Teshik-Tash cave in Uzbekistan yielded in 1938 and 1939 a child burial of the Würm I-II interstadial. Less certain is the antiquity of an alluvial deposit with some human skeletons of the lower Volga at Oundory, which were found in 1925. Aman Kutan cave in Samarkand may be the earliest dated fossil-man deposit in central Asia for populations the Soviets define as Neanderthal. Finally, in northeastern Afghanistan, several Mousterian sites of probable Würm date have been found through the labors of Louis Dupree. The cave of Darra-I-Kur has recently yielded an adult temporal bone fragment. This has been studied by J. Lawrence Angel of the Smithsonian Institution who suggests that it may represent a transitional physical type, closer to modern man than to Neanderthals.

It is difficult to generalize about the skeletal anatomy of the Near Eastern and central Asiatic people who were the contemporaries of Neanderthal man in Europe. From a cursory survey it is obvious that the specimens from Tabun, Shanidar, Amud, and perhaps Teshik-Tash shared a higher frequency of anatomical features with their western neighbors than did the coexisting people from Jebel Qafza and Skhūl. While the former populations exhibit varying degrees of both midfacial and alveolar prognathism, large frontal tori, and features of uncertain significance such as the scapular cresting and grooving (all of which are characteristic of Neanderthals *sensu stricto*), the latter populations are distinctive for those features which are seen most often in modern man. On the whole, both populations are taller than the European Neanderthals, their cranial vaults are higher, their frontal bones are less steeply inclined, and occipital regions are without the chignon and are more smoothly rounded. The series from Skhūl is particularly interesting because of its medley of Neanderthal and modern sapient anatomical features. The physical differences present in the peoples of the Near East and central Asia during the early and middle part of the final glacial advance may well be of the order of subspecific or racial degrees of variation. They may constitute one part of the species range which had more intimate ties with the Neanderthals of western Europe and another variety with closer ties to peoples in the direct phylogenetic line leading to Upper and post-Paleolithic man.

North Africa offers two cave sites which pertain to the question of Neanderthal collaterals, for both date to Würm I times and contain Mousterian tools with the human remains. Haua Fteah in Cyrenaica, Libya, was investigated in 1952 and 1955. The two mandibles found there bear many close similarities to western European Neanderthal jaws in their large size, forward orientation of the dental rows, and large taurodont molars. They belonged to a male and a female who died between the ages of fifteen and twenty years of age. Jebel Ighoud (Irhoud) in Morocco has provided us since 1962 with a child's mandible and skulls of two adults. These fall within the range of variation of Neanderthal morphology in their long and low vaults, large brow ridges, prognathic alveolar regions, and projecting occiputs. The only permanent teeth in the series are the six-year molars of the child's jaw. Those molars are larger than they are in modern man, having an occlusal surface diameter of almost 18 mm. (millimeters) across their broadest diameter. In some other respects, however, they are distinct from western European Neanderthal specimens and, for that matter, from any of the Asiatic specimens discussed above. For instance, the occipital bone is broader than is common among Neanderthals but also within the range of variation

53

in modern man. Although there is alveolar projection, the upper portion of the face is retracted, and the face as a whole is short. A canine fossa appears on each side of the maxillary bone. Reconstruction of these three specimens is still underway in Paris, but preliminary studies suggest that the Jebel Ighoud people were another Würm I population racially distinct from their contemporaries, yet possessing some Neanderthal anatomical features as well as others more often found in *Homo sapiens sapiens.*

Finally, we should turn our attention to a heterogeneous assemblage of fossil hominids (anglicized form of the Latin Hominidae, the taxonomic family to which extinct and existing human populations belong) collected from sites well outside the geographical areas we have been considering. The paleontological odds and ends of uncertain phylogenetic affinities have been thrown together into a catch-all called "Neanderthaloids," "tropical Neanderthals," "Asiatic-" or "African-Neanderthals," or even less flatteringly, "false Neanderthals." Actually these specimens share little in common beyond the few gross anatomical similarities of large brow ridges, low cranial vaults, massive faces, and big teeth. While some of the populations these specimens may represent may have existed at the same time as Neanderthals, proper, and their collaterals in eastern Europe, western and central Asia, and North Africa, other populations were not their contemporaries: their sites date to late Middle Pleistocene times. Still other so-called Neanderthaloids have an antiquity of only a few millenia, since the close of the final glacial advance. In every case, these specimens are not found with Mousterian artifacts. The real difficulty is not with the fossils, of course, but with our uncertainty as to where the fossils fit in the hominid phylogenetic tree. To label them Neanderthaloids only obscures these important issues. Anthropologists who have pulled together so many ill-matched specimens in this way and given them a common label imply thereby that anatomical ties exist and that these are highly significant. However, these same investigators seldom define the meanings of these supposed biological affinities, and for this reason they are open to criticism by their colleagues who quite correctly ask, what are the anatomical clues to Neanderthaloid status?

The year 1921 marks the date of discovery of the first fossil hominid to be called a Neanderthaloid for want of any more positive identification. This event took place at Broken Hill mine in Zambia, then Northern Rhodesia. The specimen has been named Rhodesian man, or taxonomically, *Homo rhodesiensis.* What was recovered was a skull minus its lower jaw, a number of teeth still in place in the maxilla, sacrum, pelvic fragments, and a humerus, femur, and tibia. These bones may not belong to a single individual nor to the skull specimen. While the post-cranial bones are essentially indistinguishable from those of modern man, the skull is strikingly different because of its massive brow ridges with large sinuses extending into the forehead, low vault, long face, and large teeth. To be sure, some of these features resemble Neanderthal skulls, but differences are obvious in the particular form of the brow ridges and the size and distribution of the frontal sinuses. Nor is this the kind of prognathic face that we have come to associate with the cold-adapted Neanderthals of Europe. Measurements taken from various landmarks on the skull do not have values obtained from Neanderthal specimens, and the cranial capacity of 1280 cc. is much lower than the skulls of males in Neanderthal populations. While originally dated to 37,000 to 40,000 years ago, recent reassessment of the antiquity of the Broken Hill skull reveals that some 100,000 years is a more realistic estimate. The associated artifacts are assigned to an African Stone Age tradition called "proto-Stillbay," an early phase of a lithic industry marked by replacement of handaxes by triangular points made on prepared cores. Stillbay tools were made at the time of the Gamblian (final) Pluvial until about 40,000 years ago. Formerly this period was assumed to be contemporary with the European Upper Paleolithic, although it had the different name of African Middle Stone Age. This conclusion has now been revised as it is likely that these post-hand-axe industries began even earlier in Africa. The core and flake tools of the Middle Stone Age were replaced by Late Stone Age industries as the Pleistocene drew to a close, and microlithic tools replaced the larger flakes in Africa.

Another skull with many of the same anatomical features as the one from Broken Hill was discovered in 1953 at Hopefield near Saldanha Bay almost one hundred miles to the north of Cape Town, South Africa. Although found in direct association with handaxes and flakes of the final Acheulian (Fauresmith) and with fauna, the Saldanha skull has not yet been positively dated; estimates range from 41,000 to 100,000 years. The addition of the skull to the fossil record of southern Africa served to demonstrate the distribution of the Broken Hill-Saldanha population. The series has also been observed in additional fossil material from Eyasi in Tanzania which was collected between 1935 and 1938 when parts of at least three skulls were recovered. A mandible from the Cave of Hearths in the Transvaal was found in 1947. Acheulian tools were found in both of the latter two sites along with a Levalloisian facies at Eyasi and a late Fauresmith industry at the Cave of Hearths. Again the dating for these latter two sites is uncertain, but most recent estimates are 34,000 and 40,000 years for Eyasi and Cave of Hearths, respectively. Also we should mention the Dire Dawa cave in Ethiopia, known since 1923, which has provided some human remains in association with a Würm phosphatic breccia and tools related to the Stillbay tradition. But both the dating and complete anatomical description of the human remains are not available at the present time. The Dire Dawa bones have been called Neanderthaloid by some investigators. Finally, there is the puzzling situation at Cape Flats near Cape Town where so-called Neanderthaloid bones have been known since 1929 in a Stillbay lithic context, but where the dating may be post-Pleistocene, perhaps within a range of the last 5000 years.

Just as we have seen evidence in eastern Europe and the Near East of an anatomically archaic population living side by side with populations which resemble the immediate ancestors of modern man, so in Africa south of the Sahara an analogous situation seems to exist. In 1932 Louis Leakey, the paleontologist who later was famous for his finding of Lower Pleistocene hominids at Olduvai Gorge in East Africa, reported the finding of pieces of four human skulls at Kanjera, deposits near Lake Victoria. Acheulian handaxes and Upper Pleistocene fauna were found with the bones. This assemblage has been dated to 60,000 years ago. The skulls have a contemporary appearance although they are thick and the vaults are not elevated. Then, thirty-five years later, hominid skulls were found in the Omo Valley of Ethiopia by Richard Leakey, son of the finder of the Kangera fragments. One of the Omo Valley specimens has a degree of cranial robusticity such as that seen in Neanderthals, while another specimen has anatomical features much more in line with modern man, despite its large size and prominent brow ridges. It reminds one of specimens from Skhūl and Jebel Qafza. Cultural associations here do not assist us to date the Omo deposit, estimates varying as widely as 37,000 to 130,000 years depending upon the stratum to which they would be assigned. Another specimen of modern aspect had been found in the same year of the Kanjera discovery at a place called Florisbad near Bloomfontein, South Africa. Its dating is uncertain. It may be as ancient as 47,000 years, according to one recent estimate. Other cases of modern type specimens of uncertain antiquity have come from the South African sites of Springbok Flats in the Transvaal, Border Cave in Natal (60,000 years ago?), and Fish Hoek in Cape Province (35,000 years B.C.?) These modern-looking specimens have usually escaped being called Neanderthaloid but their apparent contemporaneity with the more robust group of specimens we have described above can mean only one of two things: distinct populations of archaic and modern types were coexisting in Africa over the past 100 millenia, or else the Broken Hill-Saldanha group was earlier than and perhaps ancestral to the populations represented at Jebel Ighoud, Omo, Florisbad, and elsewhere. These problems can be resolved only with the availability of better dating information from the African sites, but the present state of the skeletal evidence demonstrates that the degree of populational diversity in sub-Saharan Africa does not become easier to sort out by assigning some or all specimens to Neanderthaloid status.

Also called Neanderthaloid are specimens from three well-known sites in eastern Asia: Ngangdong on the Solo River of central Java, Niah cave in Borneo, and Mapa in Kwangtung Province of southern China. Between 1931 and 1941 some eleven braincases and two incomplete tibiae were removed from the beds of the Solo River. All specimens exhibit large continuous brow ridges, large medial frontal sinuses, occipital bones with sharply inclined nuchal crests, and relatively low vaults with receding foreheads. The parietal bones are particularly thick. The mastoid processes are large and the massive occipital torus continues from the nuchal base of the skull to the region of the ear. Cranial capacities of the entire series, including males and females, has been given a range of 1035 to 1255 cc., values well below those for western European Neanderthals. Faces are missing from all of the Ngangdong specimens. The German anthropologist Franz Weidenreich, who described the specimens, did not live to write his comparative analysis in which true Neanderthal skulls would have been included, but from his descriptions his bias is obvious, namely that the Ngangdong affinities are more likely to lie with fossil hominids of Java and China of the Middle Pleistocene than with the much more recent Neanderthals of western Europe. This suggestion has been supported by Coon who also studied the Ngangdong series after Weidenreich's death in 1948. The taxon *Javanthropus* which had been proposed by the discoverer of the Ngangdong specimens was substituted for the *Homo soloensis* taxon. Originally assumed to belong to an Upper Pleistocene deposit, which would have meant that Ngangdong men were contemporaries of Neanderthals, more recent work has indicated that a date of late Middle Pleistocene antiquity is more accurate. The faunal associations suggest the existence of a cooler climate than is now present in Java, which lies in the tropical belt. Cultural remains are late in the Ngangdong deposit, however.

Quite probably the Mapa skull found in 1958 is of this same relative age, i.e., late Middle Pleistocene. The features of the skull cap and frontal bone, parietal and nasal bones, and a portion of the right orbital border are much closer anatomically to Middle Pleistocene hominids than to Neanderthals and to Neanderthal collaterals.

The Niah skull, found the following year, is anatomically modern. The age of its owner at time of death was fifteen or sixteen years, and it is probably male. Here the dating of the deposit in the cave where it was found, after having been redeposited from an unknown provenience in the vicinity, is well established on the basis of radiocarbon analysis as about 38,000 years ago.

Now let us return to those questions posed at the beginning of this section: (1) should any or all of the populations living outside western Europe during the early and middle parts of the Würm be subsumed under a single biological grouping called Neanderthal?, or (2) do the skeletal data reveal anatomical differences which set apart some populations from Neanderthals *sensu stricto*?

Our study of the Mousterian skeletal specimens from western Europe has demonstrated that apart from anatomical variations based on sex and age, there exists a congruity of physical characters which justifies the practice of speaking of Neanderthals as a continuous population, a concept with which all anthropologists are in agreement. To be sure, local variations were present, as one would expect in a population that covers a wide geographical range and shares a common racial history; but some maintaining pattern of gene migration between local groups must have been present to reduce the effects of genetic isolation between bands to the extent that reproductive barriers did not arise. The levels of variation we see in Neanderthal specimens in western Europe are of this nature. They are intrapopulational variables.

Difficulties arise when levels of variation of this *intra*-populational kind are not distinguished from that level of variation characteristic of *inter*-populational differences. While intrapopulational differences reflect a normal range of variation of traits shared by individuals maintaining relatively close genetic ties, interpopulational differences are characterized by higher frequencies of distinctive traits between groups which are more distant from one another in genetic constitution. Our brief survey of Neanderthal collaterals clearly demonstrates that as one moves away from the centers of Neanderthal concentrations in Germany, Belgium, France, Spain, and Italy into eastern Europe and the Near East, and still further into central Asia, we have shifted from descriptions of biological variations contained within a known population to descriptions which are more appropriate between different populations. The empirical evidence for this is the confidence with which the experienced anthropologist is able to identify as Neanderthal the skull of a fossil specimen when its provenience lies within the borders of time and space that circumscribe that population in the narrow sense. But uncertainty as to the Neanderthal affinities of a specimen found outside that circle, as has been the case with all of the specimens from Asia and Africa which we have reviewed in this survey, does not justify the forcing of specimens into a Neanderthal Procrustean bed. For example, the specimens from Spy and La Ferrassie resemble one another in a number of anatomical features, and they are identified with confidence as specimens of Neanderthal man. The Broken Hill specimen is sufficiently distinctive from both of these specimens (and a host of others) to raise doubts as to its biological affinities with them. But when we compare Broken Hill with Saldanha, we feel we have moved into a level of relationship that is closer to being intrapopulational.

Because the levels of variation are more obvious with respect to some anatomical features than to others, sharp lines cannot be drawn between those populations we identify as Neanderthals and those others where uncertainty as to their phylogenetic position exists. A good case in point is the child's mandible from Šipka which has been identified as Neanderthal since the time of its discovery almost a century ago. We have seen how similar some of the anatomical features of the specimens from Tabun, Amud, and Shanidar are to the Neanderthals of western Europe, but opinion is divided among experts as to whether the differences which exist justify placing some or all of these specimens within the Neanderthal pale. To call them Neanderthaloids would be to place an undue strain upon the premise that Neanderthals *sensu stricto* were a continuous population, for the geographical arena of their activities would be extended to a greater degree than seems justifiable for such a relatively homogeneous group. While certainly related to Neanderthals of western Europe, their degree of kinship is more distant, both biologically and geographically, than that of their contemporaries at Sipka and elsewhere in eastern Europe.

When we turn to those fossil groups which have been lumped together as Neanderthaloids, we recognize even greater degrees of biological distance from western Neanderthals. Furthermore, the interpopulational differences between such groups as are represented by the specimens from Broken Hill in southern Africa, Niah in Borneo, and Ngangdong in Java are as great if not greater than any one of these is from the western European Neanderthals. This is hardly surprising when we consider the tremendous geographical distances and varying ecological settings which separate these populations. A catch-all category of this sort solves nothing and obscures the reality of the Neanderthal population we have been describing. Recognition of the entity of "Neanderthalness" has scientific value when comparisons are made with other fossil populations. The careful student of early man cannot afford to blur the distinctions of anatomical expressions which provide the critical data for understanding the pathways of hominid evolution. The American anthropologist David Pilbeam (1970) has remarked that it makes as much sense to call the ancient people of Ngangdong Neanderthaloids or "tropical Neanderthals" as it does to call the contemporary people living along the banks of the Solo River "tropical Europeans."

Finally, our survey of Neanderthal collaterals has shown the presence of several populations in eastern Europe, the Near East, Africa, and Borneo which are anatomically more like modern man than are any of the other populations of early and middle Würm times. These are the people of Ochoz, Kůlna, Šala, Skhūl, Jebel Qafza, Omo, and a scattering of sites in South Africa. The Niah specimen from Borneo should be included here too. Those anthropologists who hold to a theory that there was a "Neanderthal stage" in the course of human evolution, of which the Neanderthaloids are the far-flung representives of European Neanderthals par excellence, would call some of these modern-type populations "transitional Neanderthals" or "transitional *Homo sapiens*." But Howells (1974) would reserve these expressions only for those populations which reveal good evidence of possessing some recognizable Neanderthal anatomical features, thus demonstrating their direct ancestry with the latter or with a common ancestor of both Neanderthals and a separate sapient line. For instance, there is the Skhūl population with its obvious Neanderthal features, albeit appearing in low frequency. He would not include the people of Jebel Qafza as "transitional" since he does not regard their morphology as Neanderthal nor derived from a Neanderthal stock. For the same reasons, Howells would reject claims that the so-called Neanderthaloid populations of Africa and Asia were transitional. Rather, he would assign skeletal remains of modern anatomical aspect to a purely descriptive category which he calls "anatomically modern *Homo sapiens.*" Those populations with Neanderthal affinities could be called "primitive *Homo sapiens*" or "archaic *Home sapiens,*" as his colleague Pilbeam (1972) had done in a recent text on fossil man. These phrases have the value of neutralizing the venerable terminologies which have come to carry specific meanings for those engaged in the problems of Neanderthal classification of extinct populations of western Europe and for adjacent regions of the Old World. Their use is an effort to preserve the integrity of the Neanderthal population as it is understood by students aware of the importance of maintaining proper perspectives of the levels of anatomical variations in human groups.

Fossil evidence of neither "transitional *Homo sapiens*" nor "anatomically modern *Homo sapiens*" exists in the skeletal record of western Europe for the early and middle parts of the Würm. This must be interpreted to mean that Neanderthals were the only human population inhabiting that part of the world prior to the arrival of men of modern aspect towards the close of the second interstadial of the Würm. Their residency had continued for at least 40,000 years and perhaps for as long as twice that period of time. Their relative isolation from collateral populations during this long period accounts in part for their genetic similarities, as reflected in a number of homogeneous and continuous anatomical traits.

Ancestors and Descendants

This brings us to the important question of how Neanderthal man is related to men of modern aspect. To answer this, we must explore as well the ancestral line of Neanderthal man himself. There are two important questions which remain to be considered. What does a study of Neanderthal origins and ancestry tell us about their biological affinities to those anatomically modern *Homo sapiens* populations which lived contemporaneously with them and to which man today is most directly related? What was the nature of the cultural and ecological settings of Neanderthals which may explain their sudden extinction some 35,000 years ago?

For thirty-five years following the discovery of the Neander Valley skeleton, the growth of the hominid fossil record took place exclusively in Europe. Prehistorians working in Africa and Asia were aware, however, that early man occupied those continents, too, for collections of stone tools found in Pleistocene deposits alongside the bones of extinct animals were accumulating in museums and private collections. All of the European fossil hominid specimens of the latter half of the nineteenth century were limited to two kinds of Upper Pleistocene hominids, Neanderthals and anatomically modern *Homo sapiens*. The Dordogne region of southwestern France, later to yield Neanderthal skeletons from La Chapelle-aux-Saints, Le Moustier and La Ferrassie, was already famous by 1868 when human remains from the rock shelter of Cro-Magnon were brought to light. A few years before the time of this important find, other human skeletal remains of modern-type man had been recovered at the Abri Pataud cave and at the La Madeleine rock shelter. Laugerie-Basse was dug in 1872. Sixteen years later the rock shelter of Chancelade proved to be another habitat of a prehistoric population of modern aspect. Beyond the Dordogne, other French sites with remains of modern-type skeletons were located. The excavations at Solutre on the Loire River during the years 1867 to 1899 became especially well known. The successes of the French prehistorians prompted scholars in adjacent countries to investigate their natural caves and rock shelters, and in 1874 the valuable studies of the Grimaldi caves in Monaco were under way. The Belgian caves of Cheleux and Reuviau were dug in 1865, and in England, the excavations at Kent's Cavern were resumed in 1867. Czechoslovakian prehistorians were very active in the eighties at the sites near Brno, Mladeč, and Podbaba, and in 1894 the rich mortuary site of Předmostí began yielding skeletal remains of twenty individuals, eighteen of which were interred in a common grave.

Certain conclusions drawn from the study of these archeological and skeletal data seemed indisputable. Neanderthal man must have been the antecedent of Cro-Magnon man, if not in fact a direct ancestor. His skeletal remains and Mousterian artifacts were consistently encountered in geological and faunal contexts that were earlier in time than those associated with Cro-Magnons. Furthermore, the marked contrast of technological and artistic products of these two groups served to enhance the glory of the Cro-Magnon people as a highly intelligent group of painters of wall murals, sculptors in bone and ivory, and knappers of beautifully made points and blades. Neanderthals, on the other hand, were considered to be unrefined and brutish in mind and body. The cultural complex of the Cro-Magnon people is called Upper Paleolithic. Shortly after the turn of the century three major stages of this cultural tradition were defined: Aurignacian, Solutrean, and Magdalenian. Subdivisions of these stages were later perceived and given names. The entire Upper Paleolithic endured some 25,000 years, merging into the Mesolithic cultural traditions of post-Pleistocene times. Cultivation of plants and animal domestication have long been recognized as important cultural developments of a new tradition—the "Neolithic"—which in some parts of the world meant the end of man's ancient dependence upon hunting and gathering as the sole pattern of subsistence. Neolithic traditions are not universal, but their origin in the Near East (and perhaps independently in eastern Asia) emerges from the Mesolithic tradition of certain post-Pleistocene populations.

Nineteenth-century scholars were unaware of the possibility that Neanderthals with their Middle Paleolithic (Mousterian) lithic technology were contemporaries of modern-type men living in eastern Europe and beyond, a circumstance revealed in our own century as a consequence of extensive research. However, these earlier prehistorians did recognize that Neanderthal man's replacement by men of modern form and different technological traditions was an apparently sudden event. Given these data and interpretations, it was not unreasonable that the conclusion was formed that Europe might itself be the cradle of man's evolution. Fossil evidence of more ancient hominids from regions outside Europe was then unknown. Some enthusiasts went so far as to pronounce the beautiful valley of the Dordogne as the place of human beginnings, the true locus of the allegorical Garden of Eden.

It was that older bias, so deeply rooted in Judeo-Christian thought, that man's origins lay in Asia which influenced a young Dutch physician by the name of Eugene Dubois to depart on a voyage of discovery for traces of early man. Dubois had read the popular scientific works of the great German evolutionist and champion of Darwin, Ernst Haeckel, who had hypothesized the existence of a prehistoric "missing link" which he called *Pithecanthropus alalus* (the ape-man without speech). After spending some weeks searching in Sumatra, Dubois sailed to Java where, in 1891, he found near the village of Trinil the cranial vault and femur of a hominid. He named his find *Pithecanthropus erectus* to honor Haeckel and with a conviction that the femur and skullcap belonged to the same ancient creature, and so indicated that this individual had stood and moved in an upright position. Here, at last, was a fit ancestor for Neanderthal man! The braincase was more primitive in size and morphology than any of those known from the hominid fossil record of that time. The faunal remains at Trinil were dated to the Middle Pleistocene, some half-million years ago.

Dubois' discovery caused anthropological interest to shift from Europe to Asia, and in 1927 the announcement was made of the recovery of Middle Pleistocene skeletal remains of man at the cave of Choukoutien near Peking, China. The resemblance of these human skeletons to those found in Java was obvious, although the Chinese specimens were originally called *Sinanthropus* rather than being given the name with taxonomic priority—*Pithecanthropus*. For the next ten years the cave of Choukoutien was excavated. It held the remains of some forty-four individuals of both sexes and various ages at time of death. Recent dating of these specimens indicates an antiquity of some 300,000 years. Therefore they are somewhat later in time than the Javanese fossils. Subsequent discoveries made in Java during the period just before the outbreak of World War II and as recently as 1969 have convinced anthropologists that the Chinese and Javanese hominids of the Middle Pleistocene could not have been members of different genera or species but rather were polytypes of a subspecific or racial order of difference from each other. Today these hominids are placed within our own genus, *Homo*, but distinguished at the species level by the binomial *erectus*.

Outside of Trinil and Choukoutien, *Home erectus* skeletal remains have been found at Lantian in Shensi, China, where a skull and mandible of two separate individuals were collected in 1963. *Homo erectus* is recognized in the North African countries of Algeria and Morocco at several sites excavated in the fifties. The skull of a *Homo erectus* found in 1960 in Olduvai Gorge in Tanzania has been dated to 700,000 years ago. Although the famous

Heidelberg jaw from Germany was first known in 1907, its dating remained uncertain for many years and it was classified by some anthropologists as an early Neanderthal. More recently it has been recognized as the earliest discovery of a *Homo erectus* fossil from Europe. Its antiquity is Mindel or possibly as early as the end of the first interglacial, a date that would make it a contemporary with *Homo erectus* from Olduvai. Two other *Homo erectus* fossils have been found in Europe. In 1959 a well-preserved skull was uncovered at the Petralona cave in Greece. While first called Neanderthal and dated to the Upper Pleistocene, reevaluation of the evidence shows that the specimen may have been a contemporary of the specimens from Heidelberg and Olduvai (Hemmer 1972). The other recent discovery in Europe is an occipital bone found in 1965 at Vértesszöllös near Budapest, Hungry. This fragment may be as ancient as the Mindel glacial optimum.

Homo erectus hominids are anatomically distinctive from men of later times by their lower cranial capacities. These have a range of from 750 to 1225 cc. for known specimens. The range values of five skulls from Trinil, inclusive of males and females, is 775 to 975 cc. with a mean value of 860 cc. The latest discovery of a *Homo erectus* skull from Java has a provisional value of 1029 cc. Five crania from Choukoutien have a range of 915 to 1225 cc. with a mean of 1043 cc. This value is closer to the cranial capacity of the Olduvai skull, which is 1043 cc. Computation of the Vértesszöllös skull fragment has led to an estimate of 1350 to 1400 cc. for its cranial capacity. The Petralona specimen is measured as 1220 cc. for this feature. These variations of a single trait may indicate both evolutionary changes and interpopulational variations among these Middle Pleistocene hominids inhabiting the far reaches of three continents. Another anatomical variable is the form of the cranial vault, which is quite low and without any forehead elevation in the Javanese skulls. *Homo erectus* from China exhibits a somewhat higher frontal elevation and angulation. This latter series has a decreased occipital breadth. All *Homo erectus* specimens possess powerful muscular attachments in the nuchal region. The chignon is absent. Heavy frontal ridges form a continuous bar overhanging the face. The frontal sinuses are large. The cranial bones are very thick, and along the midline of the vault a sagittal ridge may be present.

Few skulls with facial portions still preserved appear in the *Homo erectus* series. Specimens are limited to those from Arago, Petralona, and Steinheim in Europe, one *Homo erectus* skull from Java, the Lantian specimen, and a few of those from Choukoutien. The Broken Hill skull from Africa, which may or may not be assignable to *Homo erectus,* has a well-preserved face. That which can be reconstructed of facial architecture of Middle Pleistocene hominids suggests that the midface is straight while the tooth-bearing portions are protruding, a functional correlate of the large size of the teeth.

Apart from being proportionately larger than the teeth of modern man, the *Homo erectus* dentition is not especially distinctive. The third molar is often the smallest in the buccal series. Incisors are frequently shovel-shaped on their lingual aspects among those specimens from China. The mandibles are robust and chinless, but one finds considerable regional variation in this bone to the extent that the North African mandibles are quite distinctive in morphology from those collected in eastern Asia. The limited postcranial data is frustrating, but it has long been held that *Homo erectus,* true to his name, had a postural and locomotor pattern not unlike that of Neanderthals and more recent men. However, studies of the femur found by Dubois in 1891, as well as some other femora which he had collected but not revealed until a later time, plus a pelvic bone from Olduvai, all indicate that some special anatomical differences may have existed after all. At present the significance of these recent studies on posture and movement of *Homo erectus* is not generally realized.

The research initiated in Asia by Dubois lent support to the notion that man's origins lay in this part of the world. Perhaps the ancestors of Neanderthal man could be traced to *Homo erectus* from the Middle Pleistocene! During this period of paleontological investigation, prehistorians came to recognize the existence of a unique lithic technology in western Asia—the "chopper-chopping-tool" tradition. The products of this technological complex are distinctive from the handaxes collected in Europe, eastern Asia, and Africa. Choppers are crudely-made core or flake implements from which several large flakes have been removed in the creation of a working edge. Simple scrapers, knives, and borers occur in both handaxe and chopper-chopping-tool traditions, and in India the two are often found in the same geographical areas. Some of these crude tools must have been employed in the fabrication of other tools of materials which have not been preserved, such as wooden instruments and weapons. The chopper-chopping-tools continued to be made in eastern Asia well after the close of the Pleistocene, but the handaxes and associated tools of the western lands gave way to Mousterian flake tools, then to blades and more elaborate instruments and artistic pieces of ivory, bone, horn, and antler. These latter artifacts are the hallmark of the European Upper Paleolithic. Like his successors of the Upper Pleistocene, *Homo erectus,* whether using tools of the handaxe tradition in the west or following an eastern chopper-chopping-tool tradition, was an effective hunter of large game, occupied caves as well as open-air camps, and knew how to control the use of fire.

Before 1924 knowledge of man's antiquity could not be pushed back beyond the Middle Pleistocene, although various claims had been made for finding traces of "Tertiary Man." These were based upon improperly dated skeletal and artifactual specimens. It was in that fateful year of 1924 that the first representative of a very ancient and primitive hominid came into the hands of Raymond Dart, an anatomist at the University of Witwatersrand in Johannesberg, South Africa. He was presented with the skull and natural endocast of a child of about five years of age. It had been found in a lime quarry at Taung. Recognizing the hominid features of its dentition, Dart described it in his initial published report as a form transitional between man and earlier simian ancestors. He named the Taung baby *Australopithecus africanus*. For many years this find was dismissed by some of Dart's colleagues as an unusual fossil ape of the Lower Pleistocene. Beginning in the thirties, Dart, now assisted by the paleontologist Robert Broom, was influential in the discovery of remains of adult australopithecines at the South African sites of Kromdraai, Swartkrans, Sterkfontein, and Makapansgat. Specimens from the first two localities are larger and more robust in body form and skeletal features than specimens collected at Sterkfontein and Makapansgat, but both share anatomical features which indicate that they stood and walked erect. They have cranial capacities with means of 450 cc. and 520 cc. for gracile and robust forms respectively, and they share a fundamentally hominid dentition. With respect to the differences in cranial capacities, body-size differences must be taken into account. These capacity values are only slightly higher than those found among the great apes of the size of chimpanzees, gorillas, and orangutans.

These two kinds of hominids of the Lower and early Middle Pleistocene came to be classified as *Australopithecus africanus* (the gracile variety, of which the holotype specimen described by Dart is one) and *Australopithecus robustus* (sometimes called *Paranthropus*). They were contemporaries of one another in some regions but probably occupied different ecological niches. The large molar and premolar teeth of the robust form have been interpreted by John Robinson (1968), an anatomist who assisted Dart and Broom for many years, as indicative of an herbivorous dietary adaptation. The gracile australopithecines possess less specialized grinding teeth but relatively large anterior teeth. These dental features, plus the fact that these hominids made crude stone tools, have lent support to the arguments that they were occasional hunters and flesheaters.

With the finding of a robust type of *Australopithecus* (also called *Zinjanthropus*) at Olduvai in 1959, the discoverers, Louis and Mary Leakey, increased the number of their expeditions in East Africa. As a result, they established the wide geographical distribution of varieties of Lower Pleistocene hominids which were akin to those earlier identified by Dart, Broom, and Robinson. Several kinds of fossil hominids which the Leakeys and some of their colleagues have considered outside the taxon *Australopithecus* have been described. They gave the name *Homo habilis* to those specimens which they thought had closer biological affinities to the human line leading to ourselves than to *Australopithecus.* Much of this new fossil evidence has yet to be evaluated with respect to its anatomical variables and phylogenetic positions. In Kenya, Lower Pleistocene fossils have been located at East Rudolf, Lothagam, and Kanapoi, while in Tanzania, the localities of Peninj (Lake Natron) and Olduvai have been especially productive. Many hominid specimens of this geological period have turned up in the Omo Valley of southern Ethiopia and near Lake Chad (Tchad) in the Sahara. Some of these specimens have been defined as gracile or robust forms of *Australopithecus,* others as *Homo habilis,* and still others have yet to receive taxonomic titles, a wise restraint until such time when our knowledge of Lower Pleistocene hominids is more complete.

So far the dating of these finds can be extended to 5 million years, i.e., into the Pliocene, the epoch preceding the Pleistocene. The bifurcation of *africanus* and *robustus* lines must have taken place before this time. Small pebble tools in the Koobi Fora area of East Rudolf have been dated to 2.6 million years ago, a period antecedent to the time of deposition of tools at Sterkfontein, Swartkrans, and Olduvai. Another surprise in this recent flood of East African research is that of finding at the East Rudolf site a skull dating to about 3 million years. It has a cranial capacity estimated to be around 700 cc. This specimen—ER 1470—is distinguished from gracile australopithecines more by its size than by its morphology, but its discoverer, Richard Leakey, has suggested that it is a true incipient form of *Homo sapiens.* If this turns out to be substantiated by new data, it means that at least four different kinds of Pliocene-Lower Pleistocene hominids have been identified thus far in East Africa. A majority of the younger Leakey's colleagues still hold to the opinion that the origins of the sapient line are in the evolutionary history of *Australopithecus africanus,* perhaps through one variety of *Homo erectus,* while the robust australopithecines ended without issue during the Middle Pleistocene. Specimen ER 1470 might represent a transitional grade of hominid evolution between the stages observed in *Australopithecus* and Middle Pleistocene forms of *Homo.* There is now good reason to suppose that some fossil finds made at Sangiran in Java during the forties and fifties may be robust forms of *Australopithecus,* since morphologically the dental evidence closely resembles that from Africa. The dating of these specimens is Lower Pleistocene (Djetis). It is too early to make firm decisions about the significance of these recent discoveries.

Within the past decade research has made it possible to trace the descent of the human family back some 14 million years to the Miocene of East Africa. Here, and in the Siwalik Hills of northern India, teeth and fossilized jaws of the earliest known hominids have been found. *Ramapithecus* is the generic name created many years ago when it was thought that these specimens were representatives of one of several genera of extinct Miocene apes.

67

Only in later years did the Yale anthropologists, David Pilbeam and Elwyn Simons (1965), recognize what a graduate student, G. E. Lewis, had noted in a thesis in 1934, namely that the morphological features of these specimens are hominid and not within the range of morphological variation of fossil or living apes. In 1961 Louis Leakey found evidence of *Ramapithecus* at Fort Ternan, Kenya. Other finds of this earliest hominid have turned up in China and in Europe.

At the moment, the fossil evidence of the higher primates appears to point to the evolution of both the hominids and the anthropoid apes from a common stock represented by the Miocene fossil apes of Africa, India, and Europe. But given the poor quality of the specimens themselves, we know little about this human ancestor beyond the fact that his face is short and not as projecting as in the living apes, the canine teeth are not as long, hence the space between the canine tooth and the first premolar of the maxilla (diastema) is reduced, and the dental arch is parabolic in pattern, as it is in hominids but not in apes. The pattern of dental attrition suggests a terrestrial econiche rather than one in the trees. Perhaps bipedalism had its origins in this early stage of hominid evolution, but no artifacts have been associated with *Ramapithecus*. Given these recent developments in the search for our ancestors, it is not surprising that some writers, scientific as well as popular, have argued that man's origins are in the African continent. Interestingly enough, this was Darwin's hunch, too. However, anthropologists do not feel prepared to make this kind of statement today, nor does it seem an issue with much meaning given the fact that the fossil record is not concentrated at any one place or within any single landmass. India, on the other hand, is essentially unknown in terms of yielding up its fossil hominids. All known human remains from South Asia are of post-Pleistocene antiquity (Kennedy 1973). That subcontinent may be hailed as the true cradle of human origins once the manufacturers of India's Pleistocene stone industries are discovered and described.

Into this general framework of what we understand to be the major features of human evolution, the question of Neanderthal origins takes form. It is in the time of the Riss glaciation, and perhaps in the preceding interglacial phase, that hominids ancestral to Neanderthals might be recognized. For lack of any better candidates at present, we assume that Neanderthals arose from a *Homo erectus* stock in Europe. There is no sound reason to derive Neanderthals directly out of one of the australopithecine varieties and bypass *Homo erectus*. There are a few fossil hominid specimens from Africa and Java which seem transitional in a number of morphological features between the dominant populations of the Lower and Middle Pleistocene periods. And if it is taxonomically proper to classify Neanderthals as *Homo sapiens,* even if of an archaic variety, then the biological history of

Neanderthals is also intimately associated with that of anatomically modern *sapiens,* the dominant population for the past 35,000 years.

We know that *Homo erectus* was present in Europe during the Mindel glaciation, and possibly during the first interglacial. The fossil evidence comes from the Heidelberg mandible, the Vértesszöllös occipital bone, and the well-preserved skull from Petralona. Each of these specimens possesses anatomical features which indicate that early Middle Pleistocene hominids of Europe were distinctive at a subspecific level of variation from *Homo erectus* in Africa and Asia. Yet it would be pushing things too far to say that these hominids of some 400,000 years ago anticipated the evolution of Neanderthals *sensu stricto,* at least in any way readily perceivable to the skeletal anatomist. Nor can we easily identify, by phylogenetic lineage, any of the populations who were contemporaries of western European Neanderthals at this early time. What we do perceive is a trend toward larger brain size and a more advanced bipedal locomotor pattern where striding as well as running and walking were becoming efficient adaptations. Cranial architecture is not like that of Neanderthals. For example, the incompletely restored Petralona skull does not exhibit the projecting face and temporal fullness of Neanderthal skulls. It has some of the sagittal ridging, occipital angulation, and temporal flatness of *Homo erectus,* and as such it is most appropriately identified.

It is in the context of second interglacial deposits that we come upon cranial specimens which are better candidates for transitional forms between *Homo erectus* of the Heidelberg-Vértesszöllös-Petralona varieties and *Homo sapiens.* A focal date for this interglacial period is 250,000 years. A skull was found at Steinheim in a sand pit near Stuttgart in western Germany in 1933. While its cranial vault is low and the brow ridges are quite prominent, the estimated cranial capacity of 1100 to 1200 cc. is on the large size for Middle Pleistocene hominids, particularly if the specimen is that of a female, as most investigators believe. The face is orthognathous and of moderate size. The alveolar region is not markedly projected, and the teeth are smaller than those of the *Homo erectus* specimens just noted. It is the rounded contour of the occipital region which gives Steinheim its modern appearance. Heavy nuchal cresting of the *Homo erectus* skulls is absent.

Two years after the discovery of the Steinheim specimen, an occipital bone of a fossil hominid was found in the gravels of a Middle Pleistocene terrace of the Thames at Swanscombe, England. Soon thereafter a left parietal bone was recovered; then many years later a right parietal bone turned up. What is remarkable is that all three fragments fit together and are, beyond doubt, parts of the same skull! While there were no artifacts associated with the Steinheim skull, at Swanscombe a rich assemblage of Acheulian handaxes and other stone implements have been found along with

69

a faunal series which is typically second interglacial. While we know nothing about the facial structure of the specimen from Swanscombe, a female of twenty or twenty-five years of age at time of death, the back of her skull shows a number of decidedly modern features. The cranial capacity is estimated to be within the range of 1275 to 1325 cc. However, the cranial bones are thick, as they are in *Homo erectus* skulls, and the fact that a large sigmoid sinus is present has led some investigators to conclude that there were large frontal sinuses, as well, suggesting large brow ridges. Of this we cannot be certain. In all respects, the Swanscombe vault points to a primitive *Homo sapiens*. Statistical analysis of this specimen in comparative studies with others of the Pleistocene and of more recent age seems to confirm this interpretation.

Also included in this small series of second interglacial hominids from Europe is a mandible from Montmaurin near Toulouse, France, which was found during work carried out just before World War II. The bone is robust and holds large teeth. While it resembles the Heidelberg mandible in some features, evidence that it accompanied a more projecting face gives it an obvious association with Neanderthal anatomy.

Until quite recently, Europe provided no skeletal evidence of men of the third glacial. Between 1969 and 1971 the French husband-and-wife team of prehistorians, Henry and Marie-Antoinette de Lumley (1971, 1974), found two mandibles and a skull of a young male in the Arago cave in Tautavel on the French side of the Pyrenees, not far from the Mediterranean. The skull has a low and elongated vault and the brow ridges are prominent with a form found in *Homo erectus*. The sagittal ridge is absent and the lower face is markedly projecting. The mandibles do not share this degree of protrusion of the tooth-bearing portions. They are chinless and one is larger in size than the Heidelberg jaw. Neither of the Arago jaws belongs to the skull specimen. One of them is identified as a male, the other as a female. The teeth are large in both mandibles. The de Lumleys found a single parietal bone from the Lazaret rock shelter near Nice which, with the Arago specimens and some cranial fragments from La Chaise-Abri Suard in Charente, constitute all we have of Rissian hominids at the present time. Yet their anatomical features suggest, as do some of the specimens from the preceding interglacial, a tendency in cranial modification towards the direction of *Homo sapiens*.

It is within the third interglacial of 150,000 to 70,000 years ago that we can with confidence identify specimens as Neanderthals. Some of these are from the Italian sites of Saccopastore, a river deposit on a tributary of the Tiber near Rome, and Quinzano, a cave near Verona. Excavations at the first site took place between 1929 and 1935 and a male and a female skull were recovered. Both individuals were in the early part of their fourth decade of life at time of death. While neither specimen is complete, it is possible to

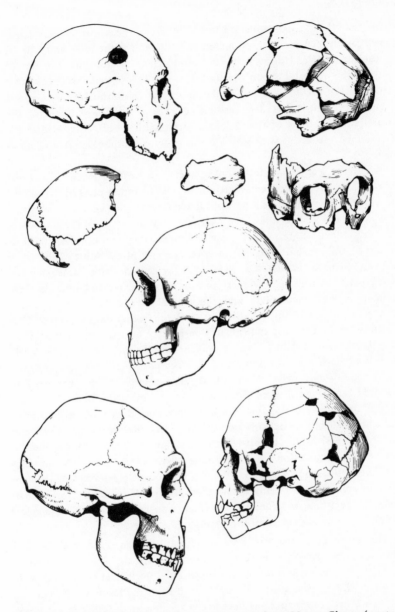

Figure 9. Comparison of fossil cranial specimens from Monte Circeo (center), Saccopastore I (upper left), Ehringsdorf (top right), Krapina (second row), Shanidar (lower left), and Teshik-Tash (lower right with right side reversed); 1/4 normal size. (From *Mankind in the Making,* copyright © 1959, 1967 by William Howells. Reprinted by permission of Doubleday & Co., Inc.)

discern that the cranial vaults are low. The supraorbital tori are very large. Cranial capacities have been estimated as 1300 cc. for the male and 100 cc. less for the female. However, in contrast to these Neanderthal features of the skull, the occipital region is rounded, as in modern man. Saccopastore is dated to over 60,000 years. The dating of the Quinzano specimen is less certain, although it has been associated with a very early phase of the Mousterian. The form of the Quinzano occipital has been compared to the Swanscombe specimens with which it shares some morphological similarities (Figure 9).

A cave at Fontéchevade near Angoulême in western France was excavated by Mlle. Germaine Henri-Martin who in 1947 found parts of two skulls. The smallest piece contains a portion of the frontal bone which has very low brow ridges and a large sinus. The fragment may be a part of the skull of an immature individual. The other specimen, more complete, possesses most of the top of the cranial vault. The internal capacity of the vault of the latter specimen has been estimated as 1450 cc. It has been described as lacking any development of the brow ridges, but it must be remembered that the specimen is very incomplete and the frontal area is barely represented. However, enough remains to indicate that a large frontal sinus is present. This is a specimen of a mature individual. Controversy over the interpretation of the Fontéchevade specimens has been fanned by the fact that they so closely resemble modern man in a number of their morphological features. However, their antiquity has been estimated as third interglacial on the basis of associated fauna and a non-Mousterian lithic assemblage called "Tayacian." Tools of this type are also found in deposits earlier than those of Fontéchevade and are dated to as early as 70,000 to 100,000 years ago. These two skull fragments, while unsatisfactory in many respects, do suggest the existence of a population which was more fully *sapiens,* in the sense of being more like Cro-Magnon and modern man, than like Neanderthal. It is in the degree of cranial bone thickness that these fragments resemble more archaic hominids. Yet these thickness measurements do not fall outside the values obtained from measurement of the Swanscombe bones.

Human skeletal remains were collected between 1914 and 1925 in quarries at Ehringsdorf, near Weimar in central Germany. The skull, found in the final year of excavation, was reconstructed by Weidenreich. This is the specimen which is the most thoroughly studied of the Ehringsdorf materials, although other reconstructions have been executed by different investigators. The skull is thought to be that of a female, twenty to thirty years of age. Lower jaws of an adult and a juvenile, parietal bones, and a femur have also been found in these quarries. Facial and basalar portions of the skull are missing. As reconstructed, it has a well-arched frontal region and a large mastoid process. Cranial capacity has been estimated as 1450 cc. These features all suggest an affinity with modern man. But Neanderthal characters are obvious too, as in the larger size of the supraorbital torus, greater interorbital distance, and projection of the low occipital region. The cranial bones are thick. Both mandibles have weak chins, and the adult jaw has pronounced alveolar prognathism. The Ehringsdorf skull approximates the specimens from both Steinheim and Swanscombe in many of its anatomical features, but it is later in time than these. It may be younger than the Fontéchevade remains. Faunal and floral paleontology of the associated materials indicate that the Ehringsdorf people may have lived in a temperate climate, as would be expected in an interglacial period for this part of the world.

Three sites in eastern Europe also have provided data concerning Neanderthal and modern *sapiens* affinities. All of these sites are of third interglacial date. Krapina in Yugoslavia was investigated as early as 1895 and work continued there until 1906. A number of skulls, teeth, and postcranial bones were removed. All specimens are in fragmentary condition. By one recent count, some 650 shattered pieces of human remains have been cataloged from the site. Some of these pieces are charred, and the question of cannibalistic practices has been raised. Five skulls are sufficiently restored at present to be useful in morphological analysis. All of these have large brow ridges, sloping frontal bones, small mastoid processes and powerful jaws. Some of the faces are of considerable height and resemble Spy 1. While the Krapina people were contemporaries of the inhabitants of Ehringsdorf, they show a much higher frequency of later Neanderthal traits. It is their presence in third interglacial times, and not their morphological characters, which separate them from the Würm I-II people of eastern Europe whose skeletal anatomy strongly indicates that they had close biological ties with Neanderthals to the west.

An endocast with parts of a braincase plus molds of a radius and fibula were found in 1924 at Gánovce, eastern Czechoslovakia. These have obvious Neanderthal features. Their antiquity is third interglacial. The Gánovce skull has been estimated as 1320 cc. in capacity. The vault is low, broad, and flat towards its posterior aspect. The occiput has a true chignon.

The Subalyuk, or Mussolina, cave mandible of the same age provides further evidence of early Neanderthals in eastern Europe. This may be the jaw of a young female. A companion specimen is the skeleton of a five-year-old child. The adult chin is weakly developed. The mandibular symphysis is high, suggesting a long face. However, there is no anterior shift of the dental row which is so often observed in Würm Neanderthals of western Europe. Associated with the Subalyuk specimens is an eastern Mousterian industry and a fauna with a high frequency of cold-adapted species. The latter piece of evidence may mean that the Subalyuk cave was occupied at a time of changing climates brought about by the close of the warm interglacial and the onset of the first glacial episodes of the Würm.

The most distinctive anatomical features of these third interglacial specimens, when they are compared to western European Neanderthals, are their smaller heads and lower cranial capacities, shorter and narrower dimensions of the cranial vault, more vertical foreheads, an occipital region which has a lower occipital torus, and a reduction of the frequency of the bunning phenomenon. Also the faces are lower. Supraorbital tori assume both medial and lateral elements. There is a greater anterior projection of the malars, and a canine fossa is present. While it is hazardous to say anything very definite about the faces of Middle Pleistocene hominids, given the paucity of data, there is no reason to assume that the Middle Pleistocene face foreshadowed the specialized facial architecture of Neanderthals. The great facial length and prognathism of Neanderthal faces are not found in earlier populations. Rather, the Middle Pleistocene face seems to be broader and the nasal root is less projecting. The face of *Homo erectus* and his collaterals differs as much from the face of Neanderthals as do the latter from the facial structures of modern man (Howells 1973a).

The postcranial bones of third interglacial specimens from eastern Europe are modern in general appearance and the limb bones do not have the bowing pattern so often seen among Neanderthals in western Europe. The prominent dorsal groove and axillary crest found in the scapular morphology of the latter population are not typical of third interglacial Europeans, save in some of the specimens from Krapina.

What can be done with this complex body of data to help us understand the origin and lineage of Neanderthal man? Even if no more Neanderthal skeletal specimens were to be found for the next quarter century (a most unlikely prospect), we have sufficient anatomical evidence in our museums and research laboratories now to make it feasible to seek new answers to these questions. Let us see how the material discussed in this and in the preceding two sections can be pulled together into some coherent pattern which will throw light on the phylogenetic position of Neanderthals, their affinities to *Homo erectus* of the Middle Pleistocene and to their Upper Pleistocene collaterals, and to Cro-Magnon and modern man. Implicit in this problem is the puzzle of Neanderthal extinction, for aside from the ungracious habit of referring to one's slow-witted adversary as a "Neanderthal," all of the legitimate possessors of that honorific exist in advanced states of petrification!

The Planting
and Pruning of
Skull Trees

The questions just raised have been posed for many years and are given the collective label of the "Neanderthal Problem." Actually several subordinant problems are included here, marking the domains of various theoretical schools, each with its own hypotheses about the origins and affinities of Neanderthals. The different interpretations are frequently depicted by graphic representations called "phylogenetic trees." Because the statements illustrated in these genealogies of fossil man are based in large part upon an understanding of cranial anatomy, the diagrams bear a sinister resemblance to those trees decorated by headhunters of Southeast Asia whose gruesome custom it was, until recently, to hang on the branches the trophy heads of their victims.

One matter subsumed under the heading of the Neanderthal Problem is the question of deciding which skeletal specimens are to be defined as Neanderthals in the first place. While there is consensus that the makers of the Mousterian implements in western Europe during the early and middle portions of the Würm are Neanderthals in the narrow sense of that term, their physical resemblance to some of the collateral populations in eastern Europe, and in the continents of Africa and Asia, has meant the conferring of the title upon some rather far-flung groups. Populations of the third interglacial have also been called Neanderthals by those investigators impressed with the similarities of certain of their anatomical characters to traits common to the western Europeans of the final glaciation. This has led to the proliferation of terms prefixing the name Neanderthal: "Classic," "Archaic," "Later," "Mousterian," and even "Cold" Neanderthals. Adjectives attached to those collateral and earlier populations exhibiting some of the characteristics of the "Classic" Neanderthals but with more modern features include "Progressive,"

"Earlier," "Pre-Mousterian" and "Warm" Neanderthals. Simply "Pre-Neanderthals" has been used in this latter context, too. The fossils from Skhūl and Jebel Qafza are usually placed in the latter category, as are such third interglacial specimens as Ehringsdorf and Krapina. Even the specimens from Steinheim and Swanscombe, while Middle Pleistocene in age, have been put under this rubric. As we have noted already, fossils from Broken Hill and Ngangdong have been called Neanderthaloids, but at this level of abstraction the concept of a Neanderthal morphological pattern seems pushed to its limits and is of dubious taxonomic value. In short, the haggle over Neanderthal membership is by no means settled despite revisions of King's original taxon of *Homo neanderthalensis* to *Homo sapiens neanderthalensis.*

Another facet of the Neanderthal Problem is the question of Neanderthal origins. While most anthropologists are agreed that Neanderthal beginnings lie in the Middle Pleistocene, controversy arises over the identification of particular fossil specimens as possible ancestors. To some scholars *Homo erectus* was the direct progenitor of Neanderthals, and the Heidelberg mandible is cited as the demonstration of this phylogenetic affinity in Europe. But to others it seems more reasonable to suppose that only some of the European Middle Pleistocene hominids can be put at the early part of the Neanderthal line. The Steinheim specimen is frequently mentioned in support of this latter theory. The Swanscombe occiput is held by others to indicate that a Neanderthal line diverged from a basic *Homo erectus* stock.

Then there is the matter of the origin of modern-type man who appeared in Europe some 35,000 years ago with the emergence of the Cro-Magnon people. Either these were direct descendants of Neanderthal man or Cro-Magnon's origins lie elsewhere. If the latter were true, then modern man's pedigree is more ancient than the period of the early Würm, and Neanderthals disappeared without surviving issue. Possible candidates for second interglacial *Homo sapiens* ancestors would be Steinheim and Swanscombe. For third interglacial candidates there are the two cranial fragments from Fontéchevade. Some anthropologists directly involved in Lower Pleistocene hominid discoveries in East Africa have suggested that the line of descent leading to modern man originated among gracile australopithecines, within the *Homo habilis* stock, or even from a more ancient population such as that represented by the ER 1470 specimen. At this juncture we might better call this the *"Homo sapiens* Problem" than a dilemma involving Neanderthals!

Finally there is the fact of Neanderthal extinction. The seemingly abrupt disappearance of this population has been explained by some as the absorption of Neanderthal bands by invading populations of anatomically modern *Homo sapiens,* a quite normal evolutionary process called "gene migration" or hybridization. Another theory is that Neanderthals simply evolved into hominids of modern aspect, a feat that would have had to take place in the very limited time period of the later Würm. Extinction of this sort is really an evolutionary transition. There is also the thesis of the complete elimination of Neanderthals by genocidal Cro-Magnon invaders arriving from some unknown cradle of sapient origins outside of western Europe. Here is a picture of a catastrophic holocaust whereby the Neanderthal gene pool was totally liquidated. This violent motif has long been a theme in popular novels and films where Neanderthal man is depicted as the stereotypic troglodyte of large muscle and small brain.

When all of these subproblems of the Neanderthal Problem are viewed as a whole, we see that disagreements over the origins, affinities, and extinction of the ancient population are based upon the importance scholars have attached to the range of skeletal variability contained within each of the small series of fossil materials available for study. This has been clearly pointed out as a fundamental element of the controversies we have just reviewed by the anthropologist Frank Poirier (1973). He has correctly observed that where emphasis is placed upon a high degree of anatomical disparity between Neanderthals and anatomically modern populations, arguments for the separateness of a Neanderthal evolutionary line are favored. Those who see only minor differences between Neanderthals and modern-type men are more inclined to draw phylogenetic trees illustrating closer ties between these two populations (Figure 10).

Let us return now to Neanderthal man himself. Since the time that the Neander Valley skeleton was recognized as a legitimate specimen of prehistoric man, scholars have been attaching him to various branches of the human phylogenetic tree. Here lies an interesting story of fossil discovery and interpretation, and today it is written not only by paleontologists, anatomists, and prehistorians but also by specialists in the physical sciences who have focused upon the problems of accurate dating methods and changes in the subcellular structures of organic tissues (McCown and Kennedy 1972).

Two phylogenetic schemes were clearly outlined by the end of the nineteenth century. By that time sufficient skeletal specimens of antiquity were present in the fossil record for scholars to recognize that they were entangled in the strands of a Neanderthal Problem. With this realization two more phylogenetic theories sprouted. Each of these four major interpretations of human biological history has supporters today, although one or two are currently most popular. The continuing survival of these theories is not difficult to explain: each one succeeds in answering some of the specific questions we face in the study of human evolution, but no single theory resolves all of the remaining questions.

The oldest phylogenetic theory, which has been called the "Unilinear school," goes back to the early days of fossil research when few hominid specimens had been found. The prevailing philosophy of that era was to fill in

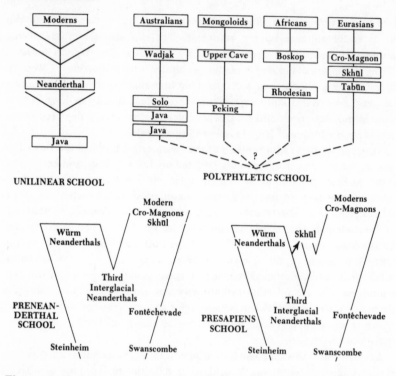

Figure 10. Phylogenetic trees. (Reprinted by permission from Frank E. Poirier. *In Search of Ourselves* [Burgess Publishing Company, Minneapolis, 1974])

the blanks between modern man and the apes with all fossil finds which could be situated along a single line of descent. Haeckel's ape-man stood as the missing link at the lower end of this line which progressed through a few hominids (such as Dubois' find at Trinil), Neanderthals, and finally at the top, Cro-Magnon and the later men of modern aspect. With the enlargement of the fossil record by further discovery, new types of early men were added to the evolutionary line, with estimates of their antiquity as well as their morphological approximations to modern man or to the apes used as the criteria for positioning a fossil on the scale. The Unilinear phylogenetic tree is easy to recognize because of its unidirectional pattern. The living races of man are often represented by a burst of short lines at the top of the diagram, which explains its colloquial name the "Hatrack school." We know, of course, that racial or subspecific variation is not a unique phenomenon of *Homo sapiens sapiens.*

Followers of the Unilinear scheme have tended to regard each specimen or series of related specimens in the hominid fossil record as representatives of a stage of human evolution which had universal implications for all of the racial varieties of man, past and present. Thus ancestors for all of mankind have passed through a *Homo erectus* stage before evolving to the next rung of the evolutionary ladder to a Neanderthal stage, thence to Cro-Magnon and other recent ancestors of modern man. Those who prefer this way of looking at things do not deny the possibility of extinctions (for where is Neanderthal man today?). But where extinctions might have occurred, that situation is always subsequent to the time at which the doomed population had already done its part to boost the upwardly mobile human groups on their way to becoming anatomically modern *Homo sapiens.* In short, no one was left out of the mainstream of human evolutionary events, and dead ends were represented as short offshoots or terminal twigs coming from the main human stem.

Both Darwin and Huxley had written within the theoretical framework of this Unilinear scheme, but it was Haeckel, in the 1860s, who first represented it graphically with his hypothesized *Pithecanthropus alalus* at the lower end of the main human stem. In the present century the Czechoslovakian anthropologist Aleš Hrdlička (1927), for many years in charge of physical anthropology at the Smithsonian Institution, was a leading advocate of this theory. His Huxley Memorial Lecture of 1927, entitled *The Neanderthal Phase of Man,* has been widely read. It is recommended reading for any student seriously interested in understanding the earlier studies of Neanderthals and the tenets of the Unilinear school. More recently an anthropologist at the University of Michigan, C. Loring Brace (1962, 1964), has contributed his interpretations of the same theory, namely that Neanderthals are the ancestors of modern man and not the liquidated victims of some sudden demographic replacement. Brace has pointed out that the abrupt extinction hypothesis has a catastrophic feature which is a survival of the Cuverian view of biological change. Be that as it may, it is not difficult to see that this simple interpretation of man's biological history, apart from its particular implications regarding Neanderthal man, is derived from the Greco-Roman concept of the Chain of Being and the Judeo-Christian tenet of monogenesis.

Shortly after Haeckel had sketched his phylogenetic tree of man's unidirectional pathway towards sapient status, he shifted to a different interpretation, one which contains some of the elements of pre-Darwinian polygenesis—the heretical notion that mankind arose from multiple centers of origin, and not from a single locality such as the Garden of Eden. This theory assumed some scientific respectability in the eighteenth and first half of the nineteenth centuries when naturalists were faced with the task of accounting for the tremendous array of man's racial varieties within the confining temporal limits of some six millenia according to one biblical chronology. The existence of separate centers of creation would permit sufficient time for environmental factors to shape the various races of man. Certain of these same kinds of frustrations were experienced by the first readers of the human fossil record, but unlike the polygenecists they did agree that all human races and all of the prehistoric hominids shared a common ancestor. *Australopithecus* has always seemed a good candidate for this position to most adherents of the "Polyphyletic school."

The essence of Polyphyletic theory lies in the notion that the living human races can be grouped into a few genealogical lines, each with its own set of fossil ancestors, but with the emergence of all of these branches from a common ancestral form. As an example, the Australian phylogenetic line might include in its fossil pedigree the immediate generational antecedents of living Australian aborigines and Melanesian-Papuan peoples, two Upper Pleistocene skulls from Wadjak in Java, then the Ngangdong specimens of an earlier period, to the pithecanthropines of a half million years ago. Mongoloid races would have a different set of fossils for ancestors, such as the people of Choukoutien, while African peoples could claim the Broken Hill specimens as one of their own. For modern Europeans, the pedigree could be traced from Cro-Magnon back to Neanderthals and their collaterals, and thence to the Heidelberg mandible. Weidenreich (1946) offered this theory, thinking that it best explained the continuation of some anatomical features of ancient populations with those groups occupying their geographical regions today. He often noted the correspondence of shovel-shaped incisors in the fossils from Choukoutien and in the present populations of eastern Asia and their relatives in the New World. However, neither he nor Coon (1962) regarded western European Neanderthals to be directly ancestral to modern Europeans. Rather, Weidenreich assumed that Neanderthals became extinct with the arrival of modern-type man into western Europe from a place of origin outside.

This view of ancient events places a great strain on the role of evolutionary parallelism, for while separated for many millenia into separate lines of descent, nevertheless men today are members of a single species. Weidenreich did not deny the possibility that considerable genetic exchanges had taken place among prehistoric populations at every point in time. Indeed, if this had not happened, speciation within the genus *Homo* would surely have taken place as isolated subspecies evolved into new species.

Coon's *The Origin of Races* was published in 1962 and is dedicated to Weidenreich. This is the most widely read statement in support of the Polyphyletic school. D. S. Brose and M. H. Wolpoff (1971) have interpreted the emergence of modern-type man during the final glaciation as the local parallel evolution of populations throughout the Old World out of an ancestral Neanderthal population. The impetus for rapid evolutionary modifications is seen by these authors as the shift in later Würm times to the manufacturing of more efficient lithic technologies and reduction in the use of the teeth for grasping purposes. Changes in climatic adaptations are also brought in by these two authors. These factors explain to them the reduction of the face of Cro-Magnon and later men of modern type, but as Howells (1973a) has pointed out, the degree of facial prognathism, so characteristic of western European Neanderthals, is not a universal feature of Middle Pleistocene populations. The Brose-Wolpoff hypothesis refutes the idea of an abrupt replacement of Neanderthals by invaders of modern anatomical form arriving from some area cradle of sapient evolution beyond the sphere of Neanderthal settlement.

Supporters of the Polyphyletic school accept, as do those favoring the Unilinear view, that throughout the course of their evolution, hominids have passed through a series of stages or grades. But the factors of geographical isolation and parallel lines of descent are the characteristic elements of the so-called Candelabra school. Adherants to both views would agree that the population from, let us say, La Chapelle-aux-Saints in France and the Ngangdong population of Java were representatives of a common level of human evolution, a stage they would identify as Neanderthal.

So long as Neanderthal man was regarded as the simian brute described by Boule and his disciples, it seemed to other thoughtful scholars that he could not be the direct ancestor of Cro-Magnon and anatomically modern man, especially as so much evolutionary change would have to be accommodated within the few thousand years of middle to late Würm times. We have said already that Boule himself did not view Neanderthals as direct progenitors of modern man. Neither a Unilinear nor a Polyphyletic scheme could resolve this dilemma. Perhaps *Homo sapiens* had a separate evolutionary line extending well beyond the Upper Pleistocene into the early part of the Middle Pleistocene, while Neanderthals and *Homo erectus* fossils should be set on separate evolutionary branches moving away from the main sapient stem, branches which withered away without issue before the arrival of man as we recognize him in Cro-Magnon. Keith (1915, 1925, 1931) was one of the most prolific and forceful writers on this theory, which came to be called the "Presapiens school," although by the time of his final year of life, Keith abandoned this point of view. Keith and his followers were examining the human fossil record at a time prior to the development of accurate dating methods. Their assessments of antiquity were based upon relative order dating of stratigraphic successions, faunal assemblages, and index fossils, and upon estimates of the degree of morphological primitiveness or modernity of a hominid specimen. Difficulties arose when specimens which we know now to be of recent date became intrusive in earlier deposits, as was the case with the Galley Hill and Lloyds of London skulls taken from the Thames. There were no satisfactory ways of determining absolute dates for these and other human bones of modern anatomical aspect. Matters were made still more difficult by the presence of the infamous Piltdown hoax, a modern-type skullcap with a simian mandible. This chimera made its appearance after 1912 and was not thrown out of the hominid fossil record until the mid-1950s, although there were anthropologists before then who could not accept the possibility that these bones and associated dentition could have belonged to one individual.

For many years before the appearance of the Piltdown man upon the scene, claims for the discovery of early *sapiens* skulls in very early deposits, even of Lower Pleistocene, Pliocene, and Miocene antiquity, had been heard. Today the Presapiens school has very few supporters. The removal of so many prospective cases for the existence of early *sapiens* by the development of more sophisticated dating techniques has meant that a once auspicious list of candidates is now reduced to what may be made of the hinder part of the Swanscombe specimen and the two incomplete fragments of skulls from Fontéchevade. Yet to the French paleontologist Henri Vallois (1958), these still provide convincing evidence of early *sapiens*. It is interesting that the discovery of the ER 1470 skull from East Rudolf has revived interest in the Presapiens interpretation. Even if ER 1470 turns out to be a gracile australopithecine of *Homo habilis* type, it may indicate beginnings of a line closer to man today than to any other progeny known to date.

The "Preneanderthal school" came into being when anthropologists became mindful of the fact that the cave dwellers of the early and middle Würm in western Europe were contemporaries of anatomically modern *Homo sapiens* settled in adjacent geographical regions. Difficulties in deciding about the Neanderthal or modern sapient status of certain of these specimens led Le Gros Clark (1967), F. Clark Howell (1951) and others to conclude that in the third interglacial there evolved from an older common Steinheim-Swanscombe stock the populations represented at Saccopastore and Ehringsdorf. These were directly ancestral to Neanderthals. Other third interglacial forms, including Fontéchevade, are the direct ancestors of modern man. In other words, the Eemian was the time when the two lines leading to Neanderthals and modern man began their divergence, an evolutionary trend already accomplished by the time of the early Würm. This interpretation is much like that of Mme. de Lumley's (1973), which is based upon the recent finds from the Riss occupation at Arago. She suggests that by the third glacial period, two populations already existed in Europe: the primitive form of *Homo* represented by Heidelberg and a more advanced form derived from Swanscombe and Fontéchevade. This latter hominid was ancestral to both Neanderthals and to modern man. This does not mean, however, that we can recognize Neanderthals in the fossil record before the third interglacial, as with such specimens as Saccopastore, Ehringsdorf, and Gánovce.

A phylogenetic tree depicting the Preneanderthal hypothesis can always be distinguished from a Presapiens diagram by the point at which the Neanderthal branch moves off from the stem leading to modern man. This ramification occurs at an earlier point in time in the trees produced by followers of the Presapiens hypothesis.

Neither of these latter two theories explains the matter of extinction in the ways it is handled in the Unilinear and Polyphyletic schools. However, the possibility that Neanderthals may have contributed some genetic material to later sapient populations would not be excluded from consideration. Replacement of populations is not questioned. What we may have taking place in western Europe is a series of local demographic replacements of Neanderthals by Cro-Magnons entering from neighboring parts of Europe and from the Near East. While this event may not have been catastrophic at a general level, having taken a certain period of time to be accomplished, its implications at the local level may indeed have been abrupt. With more and more men of modern aspect migrating into new hunting grounds, the Neanderthal populations may have diminished in density and frequency, finally abandoning their Mousterian lifeways and ancient campsites to the new arrivals. This quite normal evolutionary phenomenon of population replacement may well have occurred at different rates and degrees of intensity in Europe as it has in other parts of the Old World where populations of modern form occupied areas long held by populations of a different morphological pattern. This is hardly a catastrophic development on a Richter scale of Cuverian magnitude!

One of the last glimpses we have of Neanderthal man is at the late Würm II sites of Horton in southern France and Cariguela in southern Spain. Remains of recognizable Neanderthal skeletons associated with a declining Mousterian culture have been discovered recently at these places. Some taurodont teeth dated to the second interstadial of the Würm also reveal the close of this lithic tradition. Some of the teeth, which may not be those of Neanderthals, are found with other kinds of artifacts which herald the dawn of the Upper Paleolithic traditions attributed to *Homo sapiens sapiens.* By 32,000 B.C. an apparent shift in technological traditions had transpired in western Europe, at least in France as seen at Abri Patuad in the Dordogne. Manufacturers of the Perigordian industries seem to show a technological transition from Mousterian to Upper Paleolithic industries, while the presence of a fully formed Aurignacian culture shortly thereafter argues for the actual movement of foreign people with different customs. Their ultimate home remains unknown, although southeastern Europe, western Asia, and Africa have been localities suggested by different investigators. No skeletal data exist for this period, and the people of Würm III times are not mixed with Neanderthals in any way that is revealed by the skeletal morphology of Cro-Magnons and their contemporaries.

A part of these demographic changes of the middle and late Würm in western Europe must relate to different lifeways of the Neanderthals themselves as a response to changing cultural, populational, and ecological pressures. For 40,000 years they were the dominant (and only?) population of western Europe. The answer to Neanderthal extinction may lie in knowing about their particular cultural adaptations. These considerations are vital to any theory of phylogenetic affinities of Neanderthals to other populations, for the anthropologist must reckon with the fact that the most specialized of man's adaptations is his capacity to evolve patterns of successful behavior, the configuration of socially and often highly symbolic and arbitrary properties which are identified by the term "culture."

Any discussion of the "Neanderthal Problem" and the four phylogenetic schools of interpretation which we have reviewed in this chapter must take into account the role of cultural behavior as a possible critical factor in the extinction of Neanderthals as a population.

Ecological Adaptations and Lifeways

Interesting as discoveries of fossil bones and their associated faunal and cultural assemblages are to the human paleontologist, he also wants to know how to interpret these data for an understanding of how fossil hominids lived out their days, how they handled the ever-present conflicts of life, and what traditional forms of behavior ensured their survival. These are the features of Neanderthal man's existence we shall examine in this final chapter.

Hominids lived in Europe during the Mindel and Riss glaciations, but it was during Würm times that man began to exploit the subarctic hinterlands far to the north of the tropical belt and middle latitudes, thereby increasing the effective range of his food resource base. Neanderthal man first ventured into this "last frontier," as it is called by the paleogeographer Karl Butzer (1971), and this pioneering effort was continued by later men of modern aspect. Successful subsistence activities were achieved in these new lands when Neanderthals developed technological, economic, and social adaptations of high survival potential. The patterns of successful behavior acquired through learning within the milieu of the social group were complemented by Neanderthal man's biological adaptations to cold stress imposed upon his hunting-gathering way of life by his harsh glacial habitat. At about the same time that the northern lands of Europe were becoming more densely populated, other hominids in Africa and Asia extended their areas of activities from the long-inhabited grasslands and valley areas into the drier open savannahs and into tropical rain forests. Caves and rock shelters came into vogue as habitation sites in some regions of the Old World; earlier hominids had used them only occasionally. This geographical distribution of Upper Pleistocene hominids led to the settlement of Australia and the New World perhaps as early as 40,000 years ago.

Inhospitable as western Europe may have been during the cold peaks of the Würm stadials, the abundance of floral and faunal remains recovered in low altitude deposits of this antiquity testifies to the high biomass and carrying capacity of the forest-tundra and loess steppes. Vegetation established a permanent hold in portions of western Europe south of the line of perpetual ice and snow, for here a high midsummer angle of solar radiation provided some sixteen hours of daylight with half of that exposure time in midwinter. This stable floral covering brought animals and later their human predators who followed herds northward into the tundra during their summer migrations. In the winter both game and human hunters returned to the southern woodlands. These forests were of tremendous extent; some of pine and scrub covered two continents, from Belgium to southern Russia.

As noted already, there were climatic and faunal changes during the period of Neanderthal occupation of Europe. Even a single stadial had a series of intervals of moist-cold and dry-cold conditions. The replacement of Merck's rhinoceros and hippopotamus and the straight-tusked elephant, all survivals of the third interglacial, by the woolly rhinoceros, wild cattle, and horses was accomplished by the end of Würm I. Other animals, including bear, wolf, and deer continued throughout these times of changing climates, with deer tending to increase in numbers by middle and late Würm times. After the warmer period of the first interstadial, when the hippopotamus was fast disappearing in Europe and *Elephus antiquus* was retreating south, the onset of Würm II introduced the woolly mammoth and woolly rhinoceros. Elk, bison, cave bear, lion, and hyena are other animals commonly associated with the second stadial of the Würm. In western Asia, where climatic conditions were not as severe during glacial optima, many animal species fluctuated in frequency. At Shanidar cave there is evidence that its Würm I occupants hunted sheep, goat, wild cattle, pig, tortoise, bear, fox, deer, marten, and gerbil. The Mount Carmel caves are rich in faunal remains of species typical of these warmer nonglaciated regions.

Studies of faunal collections from Neanderthal cave sites in western Europe illustrate the broad range of animal species living in the tundra-forest and steppe regions. At the Saltgitter-Lebenstedt open-air camp in northern Germany, which is dated to 55,000-or-so years ago, reindeer make up 72 percent of the animal remains. Of these, some 17 percent were juvenile deer. Fourteen percent of the faunal series is woolly rhinoceros; less than 5.4 percent are bison and horse. Bones of fish and fowl have been preserved, too. At other sites the animals most frequently encountered are, in addition to those noted above, the wolf, cave bear, lion, hyena, muskrat, crane (or swan), duck, vulture, perch, pike, crab, water mollusk, and numerous species of insects. These findings amply demonstrate Neanderthal man's courage as a hunter of large, adult game as well as his success as a capturer of small, fast-moving game. He was not specialized in the hunting of a limited number of kinds of prey, and flesh foods of many species made up a high percentage of his normal diet. The latter aspect of the Neanderthal lifeway is reflected in the carnivorous type of wear pattern of the Neanderthal dentition. Plant foods were consumed too; the evidence for this is the fossil pollens collected at encampments. Analysis of these pollens reveals a great variety of edible plant species in the ecological setting of European Neanderthals, and some of these surely constituted parts of the dietary complement.

The sophistication of Neanderthal man's hunting and gathering activities is obvious from analysis of his lithic artifacts. Certainly materials other than stone were used, but apart from some antler clubs and splintered pieces of mammoth bone from Saltgitter-Lebenstedt, the nonlithic contents of his tool kit are rarely preserved. Amidst the scrapers, knives, and points characterizing the Mousterian tradition must be some of the implements used in fashioning these lost artifacts of wood and vegetable fibers. Probably fire-hardened wooden shafts were used for dispatching large game. The presence of stone-hafted wooden spears may be inferred from the collections of the better-made flake points. Thus far we have no direct evidence of traps and snares, but this does not rule out the strong possibility that such were used in the capture of small prey. Easily recognized are the stone tools for skin-working, knives for butchering, triangular retouched flakes for spear points, and stone balls which may have been parts of the bola. It is interesting that bola stones are not found in groups, as is the case in many prehistoric sites in Africa and Asia.

In some areas tools of the Mousterian flake tradition are found with flakes struck from prepared cores—the Levalloisian technique. As observed earlier, the changes in technology in western Europe during the second interstadial of the Würm led to the dominance of Upper Paleolithic methods of stone working, first with the Perigordian complex at around 33,000 years B.P., and a thousand years later with the arrival from outside western Europe of the Aurignacian industries. With this technological change there is a demographic replacement of Neanderthals by anatomically-modern *Homo sapiens*. Since the Perigordian is indigenous to western Europe, while the Aurignacian is not, we may have here a transition of Mousterian industries to the new traditions filtering into this part of the continent from elsewhere. At present it is as difficult to explain the technological changes of Middle to Upper Paleolithic industries as it is to account for the demographic replacement.

The French prehistorian Francois-Bordes (1953) has suggested that the best flake tools of the Mousterian were made for permanent use, while cruder flakes, being more readily replaceable, were taken during treks into the tundra in pursuit of game. At the cave of Combe Grenal in the Dordogne region, Bordes collected over 19,000 tools during eleven years of excavation. Occupation of the cave by man began as early as 150,000 years ago, and in the deposits dated from 90,000 to 40,000 years ago, the artifactual evidence of Neanderthal occupation is found. Human bones were not found at Combe Grenal. After examining this tool series, Bordes concluded that at least four types of tool kits are represented. Study of these same data by Lewis and Sally Binford (1966), who used the statistical procedure of factor analysis for the tools and their associated pollens and fauna, led them to a different interpretation of the Combe Grenal artifacts. The Binfords conclude that the assemblages are not representative of different technological traditions; rather, they indicate a situation where a single population had produced particular kinds of tools for specific purposes. They found a high frequency of tools fashioned by Levalloisian technique to be of nonlocal stone, while those tools suitable for local domestic purposes were made of stone material from the immediate vicinity and simply notched. An important point to be derived from both of these studies of Combe Grenal is the complexity of Neanderthal technological developments for tools used in hunting and camp activities. Similarities of tool-making techniques from sites in separate geographical areas may indicate communication between groups, as some prehistorians have suggested (Bordes 1961). However, the lithic composition at other sites provides evidence which is convincing to investigators who ascribe local stylistic variations of tools to the persistence of long isolation of tribes from one another. This interpretation does not necessarily conflict with the theory that particular tools were manufactured for specific purposes.

Neanderthal social groups were probably somewhat smaller in size than bands of nomadic hunters today. Australian aborigines move over their hunting range in units of fifty to eighty persons, but mortuary data from Neanderthal sites suggests that bands of ten to thirty individuals were more often the norm for the latter population. Small group size was adaptive for nomadic Neanderthals following game into the tundra in summer and back into forested retreats in winter. Seasonal movements were necessary in areas where scarcity of game was a persistent threat to survival. However, many Neanderthal groups were not strictly nomadic in the more favorable habitats of constant game reserves. One such region of limited population movement was the Dordogne Valley. Within twenty miles of the village of Les Eyzies, some two hundred sites have been located at caves, rock shelters, and open air stations. The archeological and faunal records of many of these localities show that their inhabitants were relatively sedentary, although some groups may have engaged in sporadic hunting in adjacent regions. This situation is not unlike that of the Northwest Coast Indians of native North America who built permanent villages of cedar plank houses in areas where land and marine fauna were abundant throughout the year.

Among Neanderthal bands following game into the periglacial tundra, summer camps were established in the open. At Molodova in southwestern Russia, an oval of mammoth bones and tusks enclosing fifteen hearths and an assemblage of Mousterian tools has been excavated. This outline of a tent or windbreak marks a living station occupied during a warm climatic phase. The open-air camp of Saltgitter-Lebenstedt was also a summer camp which may have sheltered several bands to a capacity of forty to fifty persons. The more permanent settlements in river valleys beyond the line of permafrost and tundra were often tents set up in caves for added protection from the elements. A posthole at the Combe Grenal cave suggests the former existence of either a windbreak set up at the cave mouth or a rack for suspending game for butchering or drying. Cave habitations became especially popular with the onset of Würm II.

Not all present-day hunting-gathering people have well-defined territories, and we have no way of knowing the extent of land areas with a resource base of critical size to maintain a band of Neanderthals. Game movements may have been more important than any conceptual preoccupation over territorial limits. Those anthropologists who favor the idea that Neanderthal territories were extensive and overlapping point to the existence of certain morphological similarities observed in skeletons collected from geographical localities of considerable distance from one another (Vallois 1962). The same point has been pressed by prehistorians noting the likenesses of some technological products and techniques of lithic tool-makers across widely separated areas, as we have noted already. Even where modern nomadic hunters hold territorial concepts, the sizes of areas are highly variable, and conquest of a new territory through expulsion of its inhabitants is a rare occurrence. Among native Australians twenty persons may exploit a territory of 5000 square miles; for some Algonquian-speaking groups in North America, a region of just over 1700 square miles may be the range of sixty-four persons. Many factors are involved here of which some major considerations are the richness of the food-resource base, dietary preferences of hunters and existence of hunting and food taboos, numbers of hunters (usually adult males), and the variables of social organization in human populations.

While some intriguing questions about Neanderthal social organization remain unanswered at present, the demographic study of burials provides a few hints about their lifeways. In a sample of thirty-nine Neanderthal burials, almost 40 percent are infants and there is a mortality rate of slightly over 10 percent for juveniles. Adults who died between their twenty-first and thirtieth years make up about 15 percent of the sample, while those who died between thirty-one and forty years of age constitute 25 percent. Less than 3 percent of the population lived beyond an age of forty years, and persons in their sixth decade are rare indeed. Most females died before their thirtieth year, due in some cases to mishaps in childbirth. Males usually lived beyond that age. Males appear in higher numbers than females; one sex ratio of 172 males to 135 females has a value of 125. This feature is reversed in Mesolithic times and is a well-established demographic feature of present day populations, as every insurance salesman knows. Mortuary and living sites give evidence of a high proportion of children. Given these mortality rates, it would appear that when the lastborn of a family reached adolescence, his mother was already dead; when he attained adult years, both of his parents were dead. Child-rearing must have been a responsibility of siblings as well as of close kin. It is possible that female infanticide was a Neanderthal custom.

But here a note of caution. Sampling error is always a contingency, especially when fossil series are small, and when individual specimens of a series are collected across a broad geographical range. For example, the skeletons of children are less likely to become preserved since ossification of their skeletons is incomplete and cartilagenous structures seldom fossilize. Sex determination in populations with a high degree of skeletal robusticity tend to be assessed as having a high frequency of males, and skeletally robust females are consequently misclassified, particularly in cases where their remains are fragmentary. Apart from thirteen adults and seven children from Krapina, none of the Neanderthal mortuary specimens are from true cemeteries in the restricted sense of defining these as special areas set apart from living areas for intentional deposition of the dead. Of some twenty burial situations of Neanderthal specimens in western Europe, only half are group burials; the remainder are isolated interments.

Causes of death can be determined in a few cases, as with the signs of decarnization of bodies and fracture of the base of skulls at Krapina. These tell-tale signs of cannibalism are confirmed by the fragmented limb bones at Krapina which bear marks of cutting tools and reveal charred areas which have been exposed to fire. The Monte Circeo I skull shows that the death of its middle-aged owner was caused by blows delivered to the right temporal region, and the base of his skull has incisive marks where the foramen magnum was widened in efforts to remove his brain. These are of the same order of cannibalistic mutilations seen in the trophies of recent Borneo headhunters. The Ehringsdorf skull may be another example of the practice of cannibalism. Violent death is observed in the Shanidar 3 specimen who was found with a stone point embedded in his thorax.

Accidental deaths have been reported at Shanidar. When portions of the limestone cave roof collapsed, the adult male called Shanidar 1 was crushed beneath the falling rocks, his bones fracturing in a number of places. Recovery from injury is also documented at this site, for Shanidar 1 had already successfully survived the surgical removal of his right arm, and healing had progressed from certain injuries delivered to his head by a sharp object. After suffering all of this, Shanidar 1 met his end standing in his own cave observing the cracks in a leaky roof! The survival of injured and aged individuals is interesting for the speculations it raises about Neanderthal man's tolerant and affectionate attitudes towards the physically less-able members of his social group. As we have observed earlier, Neanderthal man suffered from osteoarthritis (rheumatism) and from spondylitis, diseases found also in some of the animals he hunted. The assumption of the presence of rickets in the population has been questioned by Vallois (1934). The health status of Neanderthal man was probably neither better nor worse than that of other hunting-gathering peoples, prehistoric and contemporary.

Concerning belief systems of Neanderthals, three cultural practices are of interest: cannibalism, burial of the dead, and a bear-veneration cult. We have already discussed the first topic. Burials show considerable variation from Belgium to central Asia, whether isolated or small group interments. The Le Moustier youth was arranged in a sleeping position with the body placed on its right side, the head resting on the arm. Buried with him were animal bones and stone tools. At La Ferrassie, two adults and four children were laid on

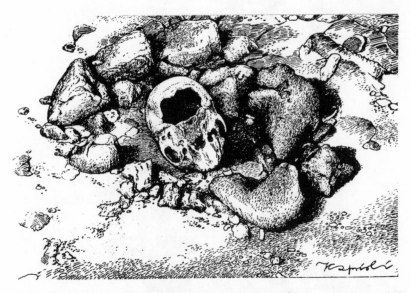

Figure 11. The Neanderthal skull Monte Circeo I, lying on the floor of the cave, surrounded by stones, the mutilated base turned upwards. (Reprinted by permission from *Hundert Jahre Neanderthaler*, G. H. R. von Koenigswald [Editor]. Copyright 1958 by Wenner-Gren Foundation for Anthropological Research, New York.)

the cave floor with their bodies oriented in an east-west direction. The cannibalized Monte Circeo skull was set on a stone floor of the cave and surrounded by a circle of stones (Figure 11). Child burials are known from Engis and Pech-de-l'Azé (by skulls only), Grotte de Antelius, Ksar 'Akil, Starosel'e, Kiik-Koba, and Teshik-Tash. The skeleton from the latter site had been surrounded by a half dozen goat frontlets with their horn cores pushed into the ground. The young person from Shanidar had been placed on a bed of wildflowers of which the pollens of eight species have been identified.

Collections of bear bones at several widely dispersed sites suggest a custom which involved the worship of this animal. Hibernating adult bears and their cubs were killed at Drachenhöhle near Mixnitz, Austria, and at a nearby site there is evidence that bears were stoned to death. This seems not to have been a simple hunting procedure, for at Drachenloch in Switzerland, a number of bear skulls were found stacked in a stone chest. (Figure 12). Here the skull of one young bear has its malar region pierced by the leg bone of a still younger animal. Some twenty bear skulls have been encountered in a pit

Figure 12. Representation of a Neanderthal bear ceremony. (Reprinted by permission from Frank E. Poirier. *In Search of Ourselves* [Burgess Publishing Company, Minneapolis, 1974])

near Regourdo in southern France. Perhaps related to this bear worship practice is the strange phenomenon at Basua cave at Savona, Italy, where a zoomorphic stalagmite is surrounded by Neanderthal footprints and small clay pellets. This was found in the innermost chamber of the cave almost 500 yards from the entrance. Bear bones lay scattered on the floor. The cave itself was an earlier habitation of bears before it was taken over by Neanderthals. However, neither this bear cult nor burial customs of Neanderthals have provided us with a single fragment of artistic creativity. The cave paintings and imaginative carvings in bone, ivory, and stone which we associate with prehistoric Europe are all products of the Upper Paleolithic and of anatomically modern *Homo sapiens*.

These sporadic insights into Neanderthal lifeways are sufficient to indicate that the Mousterians could not have possessed the primitive order of intelligence which some writers had ascribed to them. To be sure, the shape of the Neanderthal brain is distinctive, as we know from the study of his crania, but it must be remembered that man today exhibits a tremendous range of cranial forms, and head shape alone is not a clue to intellect. What is unusual in Neanderthals is the reduced elevation of the frontal region of the skull, but the significance of this trait with respect to neurological function is by no means clear (Figures 13, 14). Statements that Neanderthals were more intelligent than modern man, while not especially flattering to us, should be rejected for the reason that it is misleading to suppose that a slightly higher mean value in cranial capacity of Neanderthals over the mean for man today is at all indicative of mental superiority. Again, the range for modern man with respect to this variable is very wide, nor can size alone give a clue to one's intellectual prowess. To argue otherwise is to assume that bigger engines are always more efficient than smaller ones. Vallois (1962) has noted an anatomical development long known to animal breeders, namely that brain size tends to increase by as much as 20 to 30 percent in domestic species when comparisons are made with wild forms in mammalian groups. In other words, larger brain size is a product of domestication. Man has often been described by anthropologists as a self-domesticated species since the circumstances of human social life and cultural tradition have obvious effects upon our anatomy and behavior. This factor rather than brain function *per se* may account in part for larger brain sizes in Upper Pleistocene hominids beginning with Neanderthal man. This is one of the anatomical characteristics of *Homo sapiens* and distinguishes our species from hominids of the Middle Pleistocene.

Attempts to localize motor and thought centers of Neanderthal brains from scrutiny of natural or artificial endocasts have not been very rewarding. Only a few of the important structures of the brain are registered in endocasts. Correspondences of brain parts and their apparent imprints on

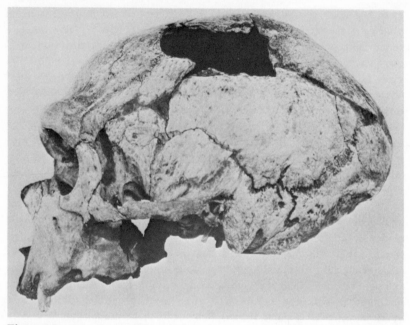

Figure 13. Calvarium of the specimen from La Chapelle-aux-Saints, France; 2/5 natural size. (Collection Musée de l'Homme. Reprinted by permission from *Hundert Jahre Neanderthaler*, G. H. R. von Koenigswald [Editor]. Copyright 1958 by Wenner-Gren Foundation for Anthropological Research, New York)

bone are seldom exact. Efforts by anatomists to localize speech centers on endocasts taken from the skulls of La Chapelle-aux-Saints, La Ferrassie, and La Quina have led some to conclude that Neanderthal man enjoyed this capacity to articulate his thoughts. Other investigators have rejected this possibility with reference to the same data!

Taking speech as an indicator of intellectual development, earlier anthropologists looked to the anatomical structures of Neanderthal jaws. The fact that the palate and mandible of Neanderthals are evenly curved along their dental arcades, not narrow and U-shaped as in apes, led to a conclusion that a larger area for tongue movements was afforded and such a distinction must be proof of speech. Support for the "Big Mouth Hypothesis" came from the observation that man lacks the simian shelf of apes, a bony strut across the lingual aspect of the mandibular symphysis which does occupy space in the oral cavity. This view does not take into consideration that all hominid palates and mandibles are essentially parabolic in the pattern of their dental arcades. Does this mean that *Australopithecus* was vocally articulate? If it does, then Neanderthals were garrulous indeed! However, it does not follow

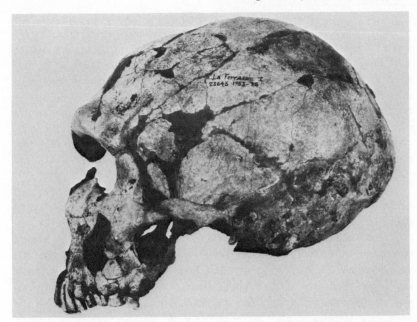

Figure 14. Calvarium of the specimen from La Ferrassie, France; 2/5 natural size. (Collection Musée de l'Homme. Reprinted by permission from *Hundert Jahre Neanderthaler,* G. H, R. von Koenigswald [Editor] . Copyright 1958 by Wenner-Gren Foundation for Anthropological Research, New York)

that a large tongue with plenty of space for its muscular activity means an organ capable of those intricate movements associated with human speech, neurological considerations aside. It is to be hoped that we shall not reject entirely the possibility that Neanderthal man had language by taking seriously the suggestion of an eminent naturalist of the last century who, when asked why apes did not speak, replied that it was because they have nothing to say!

We can be certain that muscles essential for the tongue movements of speech are the geniohyoid and genioglossal, which insert on the interior aspect of the mandibular symphysis. Their points of insertion are frequently observed in the upper and lower pairs of the genial tubercles, small bony projections in this region of the lower jaw. Since the tubercles are absent in apes (whose tongue muscles insert on the margins of an oval fossa) but are present in most of the jaws of modern man, it has been concluded by some researchers that their presence, especially of the upper set of tubercles, is a positive sign of a capacity for tongue movements related to speech. Genial tubercles are present in most Neanderthal mandibles, frequently seen in *Homo erectus,* and seldom found in the australopithecines. All of this may appear rather significant until we try to explain the absence of genial

95

tubercles in over 3 percent of Europeans and among one-third of the speakers of New Caledonian dialects in Melanesia. In these cases where tubercles are absent, a fossa takes the muscular insertions. Furthermore, these tubercles are frequently present in humans who are mentally retarded and who do not speak at all! Rather than being an anatomical correlate of speech, the genial tubercles may be explained as a result of modification of the orientation of the mandibular symphysis in cases where it assumes a vertical plane. In this case genial tubercles are present. When the symphysis is more oblique in its orientation, these structures are usually absent. In human populations today, the form of the mandibular symphysis is variable, and this is true for some earlier populations as well.

The most recent of several attempts to determine on the basis of cranial anatomy whether Neanderthals had speech has been advanced by the linguist Philip Lieberman and his colleague Edmund S. Crelin, the anatomist (Lieberman and Crelin 1971; Lieberman, Crelin, and Klatt 1972). Using Boule's description of the La Chapelle-aux-Saints Neanderthal and plaster casts of the same; comparative data of ape, modern human newborn, and modern adult skulls; and their own silicone-rubber cast reconstruction of their interpretation of a Neanderthal vocal tract, they have sought to demonstrate that the anatomical features of adult Neanderthals show supralaryngeal vocal apparatus similar to that of a human neonate of our own time. From this ingenious experiment, whereby a computer program represented the supralaryngeal vocal tract by means of a series of contiguous cylindrical sections, each of a fixed area, they conclude that:

Of all the living primates only man has an extensive supralaryngeal pharyngeal region that allows all of the intrinsic and extrinsic pharyngeal musculature to function at a maximum for speech production by changing the shape of the supralaryngeal vocal tract. . . . It appears that the ontological development of the vocal apparatus in man is a recapitulation of his evolutionary phylogeny. . . . If so, Neanderthal was an early offshoot from the mainstream of hominids that evolved into modern Man, just as Boule (1911-1913) recognized. It is unlikely that Neanderthal man can represent a specialized form of modern Man. . . .

With respect to Neanderthal brain development, the authors conclude that:

Neanderthal man did not have the anatomical prerequisites for producing the full range of human speech. . . . He probably lacked some of the neural detectors that are involved in the perception of human speech. He was not as well equipped for language as modern man. His phonetic ability was, however, more advanced than those of present day nonhuman primates and his brain may have been sufficiently well developed for him to have established a language based on the speech signals at his command. The general level of Neanderthal culture is such that this limited phonetic ability was probably utilized and that some form of language existed.

They close one of their articles with the hypothesis that Neanderthal man's disappearance may have been a consequence of his linguistic, hence intellectual, deficiencies with respect to his competitors in more recent men of modern aspect.

Some critics of this thesis have objected as follows to the methodology of Liberman and his colleagues as well as to their basic assumptions about the course of human evolution (Carlisle and Siegel 1974): (1) La Chapelle-aux-Saints was an unfortunate choice as a model for that venerable specimen is pathologically deformed and hardly representative of the range of normal variation of skulls of healthy Neanderthals; (2) certain anatomical features which Lieberman and Crelin see as primitive in Neanderthals, in the sense that they appear in similar form in modern human infants, may not be primitive in either an ontogenetic or phylogenetic sense; (3) the hospital samples of modern cranial specimens used by them are not truly representative of the range of cranial variation seen in *Homo sapiens.* Other criticisms have been offered too, and students interested in the continuation of this debate should see the reply prepared by Lieberman and Crelin (1974) in the *American Anthropologist.*

While anatomical evidence for speech in Neanderthals is not convincing to many contemporary anthropologists, some clues to brain function may be related to the evolution of the pharyngeal region whereby a wide range of vocalizations became codified into the behavioral phenomenon called language. If we consider that modification of the structure and functioning of throat organs led to other changes in cranial architecture, such as facial reduction and elevation of the vault, it would not be difficult to imagine the formation of the skull of modern man developing from an earlier skull form characterized by a more projecting face and a lower vault. Neanderthal man, whether he enjoyed conversation or not, is probably not the candidate for this hypothetical protosapient hominid. More likely ancestors are to be found in the two interglacial periods preceding Neanderthal man's appearance in western Europe.

More easily understood in the interpretations of Neanderthal intelligence are data from quite different sources of inquiry than vocal apparatus and brain form. For example, microscopic parallel scratches appear on the anterior teeth of some Neanderthal specimens. These may well have been produced by stone knives cutting off chunks of meat held in the mouth before being swallowed. The direction of these lines indicates that the food was held in position by the right hand. Right- and left-handedness is a feature unique to human beings, and is a trait associated by some neurologists with the evolution of higher centers of the brain. Speech is one of these higher faculties.

Whether Neanderthal man's utterances were simple grunts or solemn pontifications, his success as a hunter and his technological traditions testify to his high intelligence (Figure 15). His respectful burial of the dead reflects his attitudes about the value of life, at least with regard to the members of his social group. His cannibalistic practices and slaughter of his fellows are indications that he was capable of experiencing quite different emotions. In his psychic excursions between the poles of love and aggression, which mark the parameters of the human condition, Neanderthal man appears to be not too unlike ourselves in his efforts to adapt to a world where survival is always uncertain.

Discoveries of new Neanderthal sites continue to be reported (Mann and Trinkaus 1974). While the novelty of these researches and the level of excitement they engendered a century ago may seem to have diminished,

Figure 15. Some Upper Pleistocene game animals hunted by Neanderthal man. a. "Woolly mammoth" (*Mammuthus primigenius*); b. "Woolly rhinoceros" (*Coelodonta antiquitatis*); c. "Musk ox" (*Ovibus moschatus*); d. "Cave bear" (*Ursus spelaeus*); e. "Horse" (*Equus germanicus*); f. "Wisent" or "Bison" (*Bison priscus*); g. "Aurochs" (*Bos primigenius*); h. "Reindeer" (*Rangifer tarandus*). Not to scale. (Drawn by Skye Morrison, after von Koenigswald, 1958)

especially now that our attention is focused upon the latest discoveries of ancient hominid fossils from Africa, nevertheless, questions of Neanderthal origins and affinities still are unresolved. Therefore this ancient population remains a topic of keenest interest to all students of early man. Just as the announcement of the Neander Valley skeleton by Fuhlrott and Schaaff-hausen opened the door to research in human paleontology at a time when man's evolutionary history was still undocumented with a fossil record, so future discoveries of Neanderthal man will promote fresh investigations into the broadest questions about our phylogenetic affinities and about our physical and cultural adaptations to constantly changing ecological settings.

What we are permitted to conclude from our present state of knowledge is that the population designated as Neanderthal man was the dominant form of *Homo sapiens* in western Europe from the time of the third interglacial to the dawn of the third stadial of the Würm, a period covering some 40,000 years. Certain anatomical features of Neanderthal crania distinguish this population from earlier groups of *Homo erectus* and from later *Homo sapiens sapiens* populations which succeeded in replacing Neanderthals about 35,000 years ago. Western European Neanderthals are associated with the Mousterian technological tradition. Contemporary with the Neanderthals were anatomically modern *sapiens* populations whose sites have been located in eastern Europe, western Asia, and North Africa. There is osteological evidence from Borneo which documents the presence of anatomically modern man in Southeast Asia by around 37,000 years B.P. Also contemporary with Neanderthals were a number of anatomically archaic populations whose fossil remains have been found in Asia and Africa. While bearing only superficial resemblances to western European Neanderthals, these anatomically primitive specimens have been labeled "Neanderthaloids," thus implying that a "Neanderthal phase" is an essential element of any phylogenetic scheme which takes into account the evolution of the species *sapiens.* The essence of the "Neanderthal Problem," as defined by students of early man, is the determination of the phylogenetic affinities of Neanderthal man to these two kinds of collateral populations.

When some of the questions concerning Neanderthal man's affinities to his Upper Pleistocene contemporaries have been more thoroughly investigated, we shall be much nearer to resolving problems of his pedigree out of a *Homo erectus* stock and the circumstances behind his apparent disappearance at the latter part of the Würm. Already a sound beginning is perceived in the kinds of ecological approaches to the study of Neanderthal man which have been carried out by Howells' multivariate analysis of the Neanderthal face as a cold-adapted structure, and by the implications of Steegman's study of thermal tolerance and cranial form in living subjects. These are refreshing alternatives to the static and archetypal orientations of so much of the earlier efforts in human paleontology. It is in the study of dynamic changes of the human body in its responses to varied adaptive pressures in particular ecological settings that the anthropologist is able to read the fossil record of man's biological history.

Photo by Ralph Solecki of the Neanderthal skull "Nandy" from Shanidar, Iran.

References Cited

Arambourg, C. 1955. "Sur l'attitude en station verticale, des Néander-thaliens." *Comtes Rendus de l'Academie des Sciences de Paris* 240: 804-806.

Bilsborough, A. 1972. "Cranial morphology of Neanderthal man." *Nature* 237: 351-352.

Binford, L. and Binford, S. 1966. "A preliminary analysis of functional variability in the Mousterian of Levallois facies." Recent Studies in Paleoanthropology. *American Anthropologist.* Special publication: 238-295.

Bordes, F. 1953. "Notules de typologie paléolithique. 1. Outils mousteriens à fracture voluntaire." *Bulletin de la Société de Préhistorique Francoise* 50.

_____. 1961. "Mousterian cultures in France." *Science* 134: 803-810.

Boule, M. 1911-1913. "L'homme fossile de La Chapelle-aux-Saints." *Annales de Paléontologie* 6: 109-172; 7: 21-56, 85-192; 8: 1-67.

Boule, M. and Vallois, H. 1957. *Fossil men.* New York: Dryden Press.

Brace, C. L. 1962. "Refocusing on the Neanderthal problem." *American Anthropologist* 64: 729-741.

_____. 1964. "The fate of the 'classic' Neanderthals: a consideration of hominid catastrophism." *Current Anthropology* 5: 3-43.

Brose, D. S. and Wolpoff, M. H. 1971. "Early Upper Pleistocene man and late Middle Paleolithic tools." *American Anthropologist* 73: 1156-1194.

Butzer, K. W. 1971. *Environment and archaeology: an ecological approach to prehistory.* 2nd ed. Chicago: Aldine-Atherton.

Carlisle, R. S. and Siegel, M. I. 1974. "Some problems in the interpretation of Neanderthal speech capabilities: a reply to Lieberman." *American Anthropologist* 76: 319-322.

Clark, W. E. Le Gros. 1955. *The fossil evidence for human evolution.* Chicago: University of Chicago.

Coon, C. S. 1962. *The origin of races.* Chicago: Aldine.

Darwin, C. R. 1859. *On the origin of species by means of natural selection, or the preservation of favoured races in the struggle for life.* London: John Murray.

Fuhlrott, J. K. 1859. "Menschliche Überreste aus einer Felsengrotte des Düsselthals." *Verhandlungen naturhistorische Vereins der preuss Rheinlande und Westphalen* 16: 131-153.

_____. 1865. *Der fossile Mensch aus dem Neanderthal und sein Verhältnis zum Alter des Menschengeschlechtes.* Duisburg: Falk and Vollmer.

Hemmer, H. 1972. "Notes sur la position phylétic de l'homme de Petralona." *L'Anthropologie* 76: 155-162.

Hooton, E. A. 1946. *Up from the ape.* 2nd ed. New York: Macmillan.

Howell, F. C. 1951. "The place of Neanderthal man in human evolution." *American Journal of Physical Anthropology* 9: 379-416.

_____. 1952. "Pleistocene glacial ecology and the evolution of 'Classic Neanderthal' man." *Southwestern Journal of Anthropology* 8: 377-410.

_____. 1957. "The evolutionary significance of variation and varieties of 'Neanderthal' man." *The Quarterly Review of Biology* 32: 330-347.

Howells, W. W. 1967. *Mankind in the making: the story of human evolution.* Rev. ed. New York: Doubleday.

_____. 1973a. *The evolution of the genus Homo.* Reading: Addison-Wesley.

_____. 1973b. "Neanderthal man: facts and figures." *Proceedings of the IX International Congress of Anthropological and Ethnological Sciences,* Chicago. (In press).

_____. 1974. "Neanderthals: names, hypotheses and scientific method." *American Anthropologist* 76: 24-38.

Hrdlička, A. 1927. "The Neanderthal phase of man." *Journal of the Royal Anthropological Institute* 57: 249-273.

Huxley, T. H. 1863. *Evidence as to man's place in nature.* London: John Murray.

Jelinek, J. 1969. "Neanderthal man and *Homo sapiens* in central and eastern Europe." *Current Anthropology* 10: 475-503.

Keith, A. 1915. *The antiquity of man.* London: Williams and Norgate.

_____. 1925. *The antiquity of man.* 2nd ed. London: Williams and Norgate.

_____. 1931. *New discoveries relating to the antiquity of man.* New York: W. W. Norton.

Kennedy, K. A. R. 1973. "Biological anthropology of prehistoric South Asians." *The Anthropologist* 17: 1-13.

Lieberman, P. and Crelin, E. S. 1971. "On the speech of Neanderthal man." *Linguistic Inquiry* 2: 203-222.

_____. 1974. "Speech and Neanderthal Man: a reply to Carlisle and Siegel." *American Anthropologist* 76: 323-325.

Lieberman, P., Crelin, E. S. and Klatt, D. H. 1972. "Phonetic ability and related anatomy of the newborn and adult human, Neanderthal Man and chimpanzee." *American Anthropologist* 74: 287-307.

Lumley, H. de and Lumley, M. A. de. 1971. "Découverte de restes humains anténéandertaliens datés du début du Riss á la Caune de l'Arago (Tautavel, Pyrénées-Orientales)." *Comtes Rendus de l'Academie des Sciences de Paris* 272: 1739-1742.

_____. 1974. "Pre-Neanderthal remains from Arago cave in southeastern France." *Yearbook of Physical Anthropology 1973* 17: 162-168.

Lumley, M.-A. de. 1973. "Les anténéanderthaliens de l'ouest de l'Europe." *Proceedings of the IX International Congress of Anthropological and Ethnological Sciences,* Chicago. (In press).

Lyell, C. 1863. *The geological evidence of the antiquity of man.* London: John Murray.

MacCurdy, G. G. 1924. *Human origins: a manual of prehistory.* New York: Appleton.

Mann, A. and Trinkaus, E. 1974. "Neanderthal and Neanderthal-like fossils from the Upper Pleistocene." *Yearbook of Physical Anthropology 1973* 17: 169-193.

McCown, T. D. and Keith, A. 1939. *The stone age of Mount Carmel. The fossil human remains from the Levalloiso-Mousterian.* Oxford: Clarendon.

McCown, T. D. and Kennedy, K. A. R. 1972. *Climbing man's family tree: a collection of major writings on human phylogeny, 1699 to 1971.* Englewood Cliffs: Prentice-Hall.

Musgrave, J. 1971. "How dextrous was Neanderthal man?" *Nature* 233: 538-541.

Oakley, K. P. 1964. *Frameworks for dating fossil man.* Chicago: Aldine.

Osborn, H. F. 1915. *Men of the Old Stone Age: their development, life and art.* New York: Charles Scribner's Sons.

Patte, E. 1955. *Les Néanderthaliens: anatomie, physiologie, comparisons.* Paris: Masson et Cie.

Pilbeam, D. R. 1970. *The evolution of man.* London: Thames and Hudson.

_____. 1972. *The ascent of man: an introduction to human evolution.* New York: Macmillan.

Pilbeam, D. R. and Simons, E. L. 1965. "Some problems of hominid classification." *American Scientist* 53: 237-259.

Poirier, F. E. 1973. *Fossil man: an evolutionary journey.* St. Louis: C. V. Mosby.

_____. 1974. *In search of ourselves: an introduction to physical anthropology.* Minneapolis: Burgess.

Robinson, J. T. 1968. "The origin and adaptive radiation of the australopithecines." *Evolution and hominization,* ed. G. Kurth. 2nd ed., enlarged. 150-175. Stuttgart: Fischer Verlag.

Schaaffhausen, D. 1858. "Zur Kenntnis der ältesten Rassenschädel." *Archive für Anatomie und Physiologie, Lps.* 1858: 453-478.

_____. 1861. "On the crania of the most ancient races of man." Trans. G. Busk. *Natural History Review* 1: 155-176.

Schwalbe, G. 1923. "Die Abstammung des Menschen und die ältesten Menschenformen." *Die Kultur der Gegenwart* 3:5. Leipzig and Berlin: B. G. Teubner.

Smith, G. Elliot, 1924. *The evolution of man.* London: Oxford University.

Solecki, R. S. 1971. *Shanidar: the first flower people.* New York: A. Knopf.

Steegmann, A. T., Jr. 1972. "Cold response, body form and craniofacial shape in two racial groups in Hawaii." *American Journal of Physical Anthropology* 37: 193-221.

Straus, W. L. and Cave, A. J. E. 1957. "Pathology and the posture of Neanderthal man." *The Quarterly Review of Biology* 32: 348-363.

Suzuki, H. and Takai, F. 1970. *The Amud man and his cave site.* Tokyo: University of Tokyo.

Vallois, H. V. 1934. "Les maladies de l'homme préhistorique." *Revue scientifique* 72: 666-678.

_____. 1958. "L'origine de l'*Homo sapiens.*" La Grotte de Fontéchevade. 2 md partie. Anthropologie. *Archives de l'Institut de Paléontologie humaine* 29: 7-164.

_____. 1962. "The social life of early man: the evidence of skeletons." *The social life of early man.* Ed. S. L. Washburn. 214-235. London: Methuen.

Virchow, R. 1872. "Untersuchung des Neanderthal-schädels." *Zeitschrift für Ethnologie* 4: 157-165.

Weidenreich, F. 1946. *Apes, giants and man.* Chicago: University of Chicago.

Weinert, H. 1934. *Der Geist der Vorzeit.* Berlin: Keil Verlag.

Wells, H. G. 1921. "The grisly folk and their war with men." *The Saturday Evening Post* 193: 37: March.

Wendt, H. 1955. *In search of Adam.* Trans. J. Cleugh. Boston: Houghton Mifflin.

Further References of Interest on Neanderthal Man

Bordaz, J. 1970. *Tools of the Old and New Stone Age.* New York: Natural History Press.

Bordes, F. 1968. *The Old Stone Age.* New York: McGraw-Hill.

_____. 1972. *A tale of two caves.* New York: Harper and Row.

Boule, M. 1923. *Fossil men.* Edinburgh: Oliver and Boyd.

Boule, M. and Vallois, H. V. 1957. *Fossil men.* New York: Dryden.

Brace, C. L. 1967. "More on the fate of the 'classic' Neanderthals." *Current Anthropology* 7: 204-214.

_____. 1968. "Ridiculed, rejected but our ancestor—Neanderthal man." *Natural History* 77: 38-45.

Campbell, B. 1974. "A new taxonomy of fossil man." *Yearbook of Physical Anthropology 1973* 17: 194-201.

Constable, G. 1973. *The Neanderthals.* Emergence of Man Series. New York: Time-Life.

Eiseley, L. 1957. "Neanderthal man and the dawn of human paleontology." *The Quarterly Review of Biology* 32: 323-329.

Gruber, J. W. 1948. "The Neanderthal controversy: nineteenth century version." *Scientific Monthly* 67: 436-439.

Howell, F. C. 1970. *Early man.* New York: Time-Life.

Kennedy, K. A. R. 1974. "Asians prehistoric." *The Encyclopaedia Britannica.* 15th ed. 200-205. Chicago: H. H. Benton.

Koenigswald, G. H. R. von, ed. 1958. *Hundert Jahre Neanderthaler: Neanderthal Centenary.* Utrecht: Kemink en Zoon.

Leakey, L. S. B., and Goodall, V. M. 1969. *Unveiling man's origins.* Cambridge: Schenkman.

Lumley-Woodyear, M. A. de. 1973. *Anténéanderthaliens et Néanderthaliens du bassin Méditerranéen occidental Européen: Cova Negra. Le Lazaret, Banolas, Grotte du Prince, Cariguela, Hortus, Agut, Macassargues, La*

Masque, Rigabe, La Crouzade, Les Peyrards, Bau de l'Aubesier. Mémoire 2. Marseilles: Laboratoire de Paléontologie Humaine et de Préhistoire, Université de Provence.

Drawing by P. G. Wandel (Reprinted from *Hundert Jahre Neanderthaler*, G. H. R. von Koenigswald [Editor]. Copyright 1958 by Wenner-Gren Foundation for Anthropological Research, New York)

Errata List
for
Neanderthal Man
by
Kenneth A. R. Kennedy

Page 22, line 38: *For* 60,000 years ago
read 50,000 years ago

Page 99, line 23: *For* around 37,000 years B.P.
read around 38,000 years B.P.

Page 100, credit line: *For* Shanidar, Iran
read Shanidar, Iraq